THINK CAUSAL NOT CASUAL

MARKETEERS
DECISION PLAYBOOK
IN THE AI AGE

DR. FRANK BUCKLER

CONTENT

Chapter 1

THE PARADIGM THAT HOLDS US BACK 5

Chapter 2

THE SHIFT

Why we need a better mouse trap in marketing decision making 21

Chapter 3:

THE NEED

What should this mouse trap be able to do? 41

Chapter 4

THE VALUE

Applications of Causal AI in marketing 83

Chapter 5

THE DOING

How you can win over your organization for this task 119

Chapter 6

THE "SO WHAT"

Why, how and when to start 135

ABOUT THE AUTHOR 139

Chapter 1

THE PARADIGM THAT HOLDS US BACK

It was the summer of 1998 and I was about to graduate with a degree in electrical engineering and marketing. I received a precious invitation letter from McKinsey and it made my heart happy. A one-day talent event where we were to get to know the company through case studies. At the last minute, I bought myself an expensive yellow tie that would go well with my green suit. It was probably the color choice that disqualified me as unsuitable for McKinsey. But what I remember from this event were the case studies.

The room was full of "high performers" from all areas. Everyone was handed a case study description and we had 15 minutes to solve it. Specifically, it was described how many "MJ" the consultancy has available to help a company. "MJ" was a German abbreviation used by consultants for "man years of work".

Then came the bang. Mark was the first to present his result. He was a budding physicist and began with his solution: "According to my calculations, we have gained 23 million watts". We all sat there open-mouthed, including the McKinsey consultants. "What is he talking about?" was written above our heads. It turned out that the case study abbreviated "man-years" to MJ and that MJ stands for mega joules in physics. The eager Mark had taken the DATA for what he thought it was ... and produced nonsense. He himself seemed to think this was plausible, as he was the first to point it out.

"Data is gold" is a frequently used metaphor. Mark couldn't do anything with the "gold". Why not? Because the metaphor is misleading.

Data is more like atoms. Humans consist of 99 percent carbon, hydrogen and oxygen atoms. If we were to place these atoms neatly separated "in three piles", it would be impossible to build a human being from them.

Data are building blocks, but the magic in the context is not in the data. The magic is in the MEANING of the data. That's what this book is about and what that means for the marketing management of companies.

The magic of data analysis lies in the context of meaning. However, the prevailing understanding in marketing management is more like this:

- Collect lots of data - this is based on the belief that the more "data" you have, the more "knowledge" you can gain from it.

- Give the data to the analysis nerds and the PhD's. They're the ones with the glasses. Down there in the basement, where they sit, they will use them to do a lot of calculations and produce insights.
- Then you look at the results and if they are not plausible, you send the geeks back to the basement.

This understanding is not only very one-eyed, but also dangerous. With this book, I would like to contribute to a more enlightened and effective use of data for business decisions.

Architects, not just construction workers

Let me illustrate this with a specific example. Many years ago, I was invited by a coffee brand that sells its products through direct sales. They were looking for a data analytics consultant to help them with customer churn. The Head of Customer Relationship Management got straight to the point with his first slide: "Here's our data. Your job is to find out for us who will be churning.

In five steps, it should become clear that the task was formulated somewhat shortsightedly.

The very first question that did not arise from the data was: "What is a churned customer? Because the brand did not have a subscription model. The customers merely showed irregular ordering behavior. We therefore decided to predict the time until the next order rather than the "churn".

The next question to be answered was which data should be used as input. Of course, you could simply take "all" the data that belongs to a customer. But a customer sometimes has a long history.

How relevant is the purchase data from 3 years ago for today's customer churn? It turns out that you can achieve better results faster with "common sense".

Then there is data that describes the context or situation and does not belong directly to the customer. Seasonality, weather, advertising activities and much more can influence customer behavior. Much of this data can be obtained with limited effort, but is not contained in the data set described as "huge". Again, it is the technical understanding, not the analytical expertise, that makes the analysis successful.

But the story goes even further. With the "right" input data and the appropriate target variable (time until the next order), we were now able to train a state-of-the-art machine learning model that estimated the order time with astonishing accuracy.

Nevertheless, it became clear that this approach was still largely missing the mark. After all, it was of course much more important for the coffee brand not to lose customers with high turnover. In this respect, the target function "predicting the next order" was not aligned with the actual goal of "avoiding loss of sales".

One way of dealing with this is to weight the data records according to their customer value in the machine learning process. A machine learning method that allows this must be used.

Here, too, an understanding of the content of the actual objectives is necessary in order to align the analysis method with them. This understanding is not present in the data.

This case study has not yet been completed.

The machine learning model now predicts the time until the next order. Because the customers with higher sales now have a greater weight, the forecasts for customers with lower sales have a higher error than those for customers with high sales.

What do we do with this forecast? We can filter out the customers with a very high "time to next order" value and reward them with customer loyalty measures. But what threshold should we use? Again, a question that the data does not answer.

Looking at the two errors (so-called alpha and beta errors) quickly makes this clear. Figure 1 illustrates this. It will happen that the forecast selects a customer as a "churner" on the basis of the threshold value, but this customer is not actually a churner. This is a clear "false alarm". The cost of this error is that the customer retention campaign would not have been necessary for this person. In the case of the coffee brand, the costs was 20 euros.

The second error is that a customer is not selected in the forecast, even though he will be a churned customer. The cost of this error is the customer value of the lost customer multiplied by the probability of success of the loyalty measure. For the coffee brand, this was an average of 240 euros multiplied by the probability of success of 30% equals 80 euros.

When I talk to marketing managers about churn, I often hear statements like: "We have a hit rate of 90%. That's not bad, is it? In fact, the hit rate is a meaningless figure.

Why is that the case? It's not about how many churners and non-churners are recognized. What matters is that the expensive errors are avoided. In our case, not detecting churners was four times as expensive as a false alarm.

We therefore chose the threshold value in such a way that opportunity costs are minimized by applying enough customer loyalty measures.

Let me summarize. It was essential to incorporate management context knowledge in at least 5 places.

1. the task itself was wrong. The task should not be to predict which customer will churn. Rather, the task is to manage customer retention measures in an ROI-optimized way. That is a huge difference.

2. It was a question of content as to which customer is now considered to have churned. Here we opted for a non-binary target value. In other

words, we decided against categorizing customers as "churned", as this is not known in reality.

3. even the selection of data, which is necessary due to the long customer history, was a question of expert judgment. It turned out that central, situational information that influences success still had to be developed.

4. it turned out that it is necessary to weight the analysis with customer value to ensure that the machine learning algorithms pursue the same goals as marketing management.

5 Finally, the threshold for the churn classification and the customer retention campaign was chosen to optimize ROI and not the hit rate.

All this expert knowledge, which made the results successful, did not essentially require data science knowledge.

	Prediction below threshold	Prediction above threshold
Actual below threshold	Hit	False Alarm
Actual above threshold	Lost Revenue	Hit

Sometimes a picture is worth a thousand words. Do you know the following situation too? You go to the garage because something is squeaking on your car. The mechanic thinks the shock absorbers need replacing. "The tires should also be replaced" he says "and the wiper fluid with anti-freeze too".

None of what he recommends is wrong per se. But you are only concerned about driving safety and not about squeaking. You don't need antifreeze in your region because you don't want to drive in the mountains. You only drive your car occasionally and the tires would certainly last another two years.

It's your car and only you know what to do with it and what you want with it. No mechanic can do that for you.

A more controversial but all the more fitting image is that of a physician. Some people go to the doctor and blindly follow his recommendations. They take symptom-relieving medication without realizing that it is usually counterproductive for the healing process.

Every medical treatment has an alpha and a beta error. Every medical treatment has the risk of side effects (analogous to the cost of a churn measure) and the risk of disease consequences if not treated.

Who should weigh up these two errors? The doctor or the patient?

Experts tend to throw smoke and mirrors with their profound specialist knowledge. They have an unconscious interest in underpinning their raison d'être. They know a thousand problems and reasons why simple strategies are problematic.

Data scientists are no different. That is why marketing management that takes responsibility is crucial for success.

What do you think? Would an engineer 100 years ago have come up with the idea of offering a Ford Model T that the customer couldn't configure?

"You can have any color as long as it's black," Henry Ford is quoted as saying.

Only through standardization was it possible to produce a car that everyone could afford. I am sure that the engineers must have dismissed this crazy idea as absurd at the time.

Your data science engineers need your guidance, just like Henry Ford's engineers needed it. Data is not gold. They are building blocks. Architects need builders to build a beautiful house out of them.

Marketing managers must take responsibility

In addition to the myth that "data is gold", I am also experiencing another, unhelpful school of thought at board level.

The "management by plausibility" principle works like this: look at the results of the data scientists and if they are not plausible, send the "geeks back to the basement".

I had my own personal aha moment when I was in charge of a sales team in Corporate America almost twenty years ago. Every month, I sat with the sales managers to look at the figures in the "Performance Review".

"Why has sales in this region slumped here?" I asked Joachim. He expanded and told me three very plausible details about customers who had probably been the main contributors. Suddenly I realized that the data filter had accidentally been set to the previous year. I changed it and suddenly there was an increase in turnover. Joachim took a quick breath and began with three very clear developments that justified these figures.

I realized that the main part of leadership work consisted of listening to the stories of subordinates, checking them for plausibility and providing further impetus for action.

The more I thought about it, the more I realized that plausibility is not a particularly good indicator of truth. It only says something about whether a story fits in with previous beliefs. Plausible stories can be true. But there is a considerable probability that they are "absolute nonsense".

Implausible stories can also be true. In fact, the most groundbreaking discoveries are "implausible" because they contradict previous false beliefs.

The same applies to data science. Marketing management should not see itself as a reactive controller. Rather, the expertise of the marketing department is the decisive input for successful data analysis and not just a control instance.

Data alone is "nothing". Without data, everything is nothing. Artificial intelligence can create value from data. But only if it is steered in the right direction by human expertise.

To use a metaphor, "management by plausibility" is like a mute restaurant customer. Someone chooses the food for them, and all they can do is spit it out again if they don't like it.

The new model is the restaurant guest who chooses his own food. They do not have to be able to cook themselves. However, knowledge of the ingredients is helpful. This way, the guest can not only be sure that the food tastes good. They can also ensure that it is healthy and therefore meets their expectations.

Of course, an uneducated restaurant guest who only knows fast food will hardly be able to intervene. But that's life. You don't have to be an expert in everything. But it helps to take responsibility for your life, your body and your relationships and to acquire a little wisdom about everything.

Marketing experts should behave in the same way. Take responsibility and ensure that data science moves in the right direction.

Data scientists are not the problem

This is not to say that data science per se is going in the wrong direction or that they are "simple-minded technical idiots". Quite the opposite. Many are doing a great job. Many save what management fails to do.

But relying on that is negligent. It's like getting into a cab and trusting that the driver already knows where he's going. If in doubt, the cab driver will go where he wants to go.

From correlation to causality

The scandals surrounding discriminatory machine learning models are another example of how central the framework conditions that you set as management are.

A prominent example of discrimination through machine learning is a large bank's lending system. Research showed that this system systematically disadvantaged applicants from certain ethnic minorities by offering them poorer credit terms or rejecting their applications more frequently, even if their financial situation was comparable to that of preferred groups.

Another case relates to criminal recidivism prediction software used in the US justice system. Investigations revealed that this system falsely classified blacks as future recidivists significantly more often than whites, although this was not the case with otherwise identical criminal histories.

The reason for this discrimination is a misunderstanding that even many experienced data scientists still fall prey to. They train a machine learning model with as many descriptive features as possible (e.g. skin color) in order to then predict a target feature (e.g. credit default). The problem with this is that the descriptive characteristics are often related and therefore correlated. For example, people with white skin color tend to have a higher salary due to other background variables.

Although salary is the actual cause of creditworthiness, many machine learning algorithms also use information about skin color. "As long as the prediction error in the data is small" is the algorithms' motto.

However, the motto should be: "The main thing is that the information used is causal". This motto will guide us throughout this book. It is the guiding principle of all causal AI methods. We will see how it leads not only to non-discriminatory models, but also to more stable and better models.

Lottery companies are usually convinced, based on their data analysis, that their target group is older people. This conclusion is drawn because we tend to equate correlation with causation. Conventional machine learning approaches do this too - only in a multidimensional space.

Smart managers question this. The application of Causal AI to data from a lottery company revealed a different picture. All other things being equal, older people are less likely to start playing the lottery. Nevertheless, it is a fact that older people play the lottery more.

Causal AI clarified the paradox. Over the course of time (i.e. years of life), people get used to playing the lottery. The more you play, the more likely you are to win at times. This winning experience in turn increases customer loyalty. Similar to the discriminatory models, it is not a personal characteristic (age) but certain customer experiences that determine their behavior.

The consequences of this realization for management could not be greater. The target group is the young, not the old. The aim is to habituate customers, not to increase casual play by offering jackpots. Frequent winning experiences keep players interested, while offering jackpots leads to customers playing less often and waiting until the money pot is full again.

The other day I wanted to play soccer outside with my two children. I looked out onto the terrace. It was wet. "Boys, we can't play, it's raining," I said. My boys were not happy with my announcement and stormed out onto the patio. "It's not raining," they said.

Indeed. I had behaved like many data scientists and many managers. I had confused correlation with causality. The terrace was still wet from the morning's rain. But now it hadn't just stopped raining. The cloud cover had even cleared.

Similarly, conventional machine learning algorithms like to use surrogate information to predict target values. In practice, this approach only works by chance.

What do we learn from this?

On my way to the office in the morning, I usually stop at an Italian coffee cart and strike up a conversation with other guests. When asked "What do you do for a living?", I usually answer "My company extracts insights from data using artificial intelligence". Most people then say that I work in the "IT industry", which always confuses me.

The situation is similar with data analysis in companies. When it comes to analyzing data, you either think of computer scientists or data scientists. But let's be honest. What job these days doesn't involve data? What job can do without computers? If my grandfather were still alive, he would describe my job as "something to do with computers".

My outcry in this book is to understand the profession of marketing managers in such a way that they also take responsibility for analyzing their data and managing its outcomes. For this task, I would like to show in this book what you should think about in order to make effective, data-based decisions.

You don't need to have studied medicine to become an empowered patient. It's enough to internalize a few guidelines and ask the right questions. For example, when I meet my physician, I ask her

- Does this medication combat the cause or the symptom?
- How do the side effects (alpha error) compare with the possible consequences of not taking the medication (beta error)?
- What are the consequences if I postpone the decision (wait-and-see strategy)?
- How would you decide if you were me?

I inform the doctors about my goals (e.g. avoiding suffering or accepting suffering if it benefits my health in the long term). It turns out that many doctors can deal well with mature patients.

This can also happen to data scientists. "When you have a hammer, every problem looks like a nail". If your requirements don't fit into the in-house data scientist's toolbox, there may be a need to talk.

Some doctors use a lot of technical terms and a lot of Latin. A data scientist could try to get rid of you just as eloquently. That's why rule number one applies: if something is not understandable, just ask "stupid" questions.

Another analogy from the world of medicine should encourage you to do so. In medical school and in medical practice, 99 percent of the focus is on curing diseases and serious illnesses. This great expertise is there to cure diseases. However, when it comes to the question of how to maintain health and physical resilience, the discipline has its blind spots.

So don't assume that a data scientist will gain the best possible insights from your data just because they have a doctorate in this field.

I therefore repeat once again: for you as a marketing manager, data analysis is YOUR job. Because data analysis today means nothing other than "learning from experience". What you learn in your field should be important to you. You should not leave it to a black box.

Key Learning

- *Marketing expertise is the key design component of data analysis.*

- *Equating correlation and causality is the cardinal error that unites management and data science to this day.*

Chapter 2

THE SHIFT -

Why we need a better mouse trap in marketing decision making

What management and data science still have in common today is that they rarely distinguish between correlation and causality.

Sonos analyzed the feedback data that came from the owners of the speakers. The first step was the correlation analysis. It's hard to believe: the willingness to recommend correlated most strongly with service satisfaction. Was the hotline really the success factor?

A more appropriate analysis (we will get to know it later) showed that new customers in particular were more willing to recommend the company to others due to the initial euphoria. However, the customer hotline was primarily used by new customers, as this is where most questions about setting up the devices arose. The service contacts therefore proved to be the second consequence of new customer acquisition. As a result, the willingness to recommend correlated with service satisfaction, as it was a consequence of new customer acquisition. However, there was no causal relationship.

Limits of conventional methods

These and other examples show one thing: correlation analysis is not suitable for tracking down causes. What methods has statistics or, as we say today, data science developed for this? These are, for example, econometric models and structural equation models. Let's look at an example to see how useful these methods are in practice.

The company Mintel collects data on new products worldwide. In fact, thousands of employees "roam" through supermarkets worldwide to find new products, evaluate them subjectively and send them to the headquarters in London, where they are objectively evaluated and categorized. Sales figures, distribution figures, prices and lots of other data are collected in a huge database for this purpose.

From time to time, the experts ask bold questions like these: Why do only 5% of all new product launches survive the first two years? How can I predict whether my product will be successful? How can I manage it at an early stage?

So the company's data scientists set about unearthing the treasure trove of data. An econometric model was built. It was tweaked and tinkered with. But the explanatory power was more than sobering:

ZERO

Then one day I received this email asking if we had any better methods.

We had them. Once the work was done, we were able to predict with 81% accuracy whether each new product would be a winner or a loser.

How was that possible? Is classical modeling really that "bad"?

No, "bad" is the wrong word. Classic modeling is not practicable. It does not have the methodological properties that AI offers us today and that it needs in order to gain useful insights in a predictable manner within a limited time.

Specifically, there are problems in the following three areas in particular

1. Hypothesis-based

Even in classical research today, it is still considered the gold standard to always proceed on the basis of hypotheses. Most of us learned this in our studies. The reason behind this is that (without using the methods we will get to know) only a good hypothesis actually prevents a spurious correlation from being declared true, i.e. causal.

The only practical problem is that there is usually a lack of good hypotheses. The greater the need for useful insights, the fewer hypotheses are available. The more reliable hypotheses there are, the more likely marketers are to say to themselves: Well, what we know is enough for us to make decisions. This is always referred to as the "last digit after the decimal point that you don't need".

Collecting hypotheses with the help of expert interviews is really a lot of work and takes time. Nevertheless, there are still gaps, large gaps. Forming hypothesis leads to small statistical explanatory models because there are typically only a few reliable hypotheses left. These small models explain less. What is even worse, however, is that they are associated with an invisibly higher risk of delivering false results. We will see why this is the case later in the context of "confounders".

So both in practice and in science, people "cheat" behind the scenes. You simply look at the data you have and see if you can come up with a hypothesis. The proper procedure would be the other way around.

It is not uncommon for hypotheses to be "knitted" after the analysis. The whole thing is then idealized as the fine art of "storytelling".

It was the same with Mintel. "All variables in" and then "let's see". Even the statement of the customers surveyed as to whether they would buy a product or not had no explanatory power for the product's success.

Does this disprove the hypothesis that a higher purchase intention also leads to purchases?

Yes and no. Assuming that all model assumptions are correct, yes. This brings us to the second point.

2. Linear and independent

For example, many new products are more likely to be considered if they are perceived as unique. However, it turns out that uniqueness can be overdone. "Very unique" becomes "quite strange".

The standard methods of classical modeling assume that the more pronounced an explanatory variable is (e.g. the more unique), the greater the target variable (e.g. the sales figures of the product). A fixed relationship is assumed. It is a linear relationship. Only the extent of the relationship is determined by the parameters.

The second standard assumption is independence. According to this, a price reduction of 1 euro, for example, has a certain absolute sales effect of, say, 50%. - regardless of the brand of the product, for example. Even if this does not seem very realistic in this example, it is the core of all standard methods. Sure, with econometric methods, it is possible to make them non-linear. It is also possible to map the dependencies between the causes in the model. There's just one catch: it's hypothesis-based. You have to know it in advance.

The data scientist needs to know what kind of non-linearity to build in. Is it a saturation function? A U-function? A growth function? An S-function?

He also needs to know what kind of dependency he should "build in". Do we have an AND link, i.e. sales only increase if the price falls AND the brand is strong? Or an OR link? Or an EITHER link? Or something in between?

The MINTEL model had 200 variables. Even if you only have 100 variables, the question arises: Who goes through them all to correctly determine the non-linearity? And who goes through all 100 times 100 (=10,000) combinations to see how they are related and interact?

This makes it plausible how impractical classical statistical modeling is. The methods should help us to learn what we do not yet know and not just validate what we already know.

Number of variables and different scales

There are other challenges in business practice where traditional methods fail.

Imagine painting a 10 cm long line on a sheet of paper with a brush. Then paint an area of 10 x 10 cm with it. How much paint do you need? If you have a thick brush, perhaps ten times as much. Now we go from two-dimensional to three-dimensional. How much paint do we need to fill a 10 x 10 x 10 cm box with paint?

The paint is the data we need. The dimensions are the variables we have. The point is this: the more explanatory variables we have, the larger the space of possibilities. This space contains our data. As the number of variables increases, we theoretically need exponentially more data. This phenomenon is known as the "curse of dimensionality".

The only tools that classical methods use to overcome the curse of dimensionality are hypotheses and assumptions. We have seen that this is not very practical.

In the course of the development of artificial intelligence, intelligent methods have been developed that get to grips with the curse of dimensionality without strict hypotheses and assumptions.

For example, when AI algorithms today identify a cat in an image with 1000 x 1000 pixels, they process 1 million (1000 x 1000) explanatory variables. The possibility space here is significantly larger than the sum of the elementary particles in the entire universe (10^{81}) could fill. Even the millions of cats that the algorithm has seen are a drop in the ocean.

Highly dimensional challenges in corporate marketing can be mapped in the same way.

Another limitation of classic modeling is the use of differently scaled variables. There are binary variables such as gender or segment affiliation. And there are continuous variables such as customer satisfaction or turnover. Classical statistics can hardly mix these.

The data sets are therefore divided e.g. into women and men, estimated separately and then compared. The sample is thus halved, as is the significance, and the gender analysis is purely correlative (instead of causal).

The requirements in business practice are different. But if you only have a hammer, every problem looks like a nail.

This was also the case in the Mintel project. If classical modeling is hypothesis-based and postulates linearity and independence of effects, it is intuitively plausible that the approach has its limitations. This becomes even clearer when we look at what a modern AI-based method has found:

The central insight of the model is that the success levers are mutually dependent. To sell a product, it has to be on the shelf. A good-looking product is useless if the degree of distribution is low. A high level of distribution is useless if the product is not so good that consumers want to buy it again. A good product is useless if the price is not within an acceptable range. An acceptable price is of no use if the brand is not recognized on the shelf. All these factors are interdependent rather than complementary.

Generate 100 random numbers between 0 and 1 for 4 variables. For each of these 4 number series, half of the cases are greater than 0.5. If you multiply two of the variables (number series), only 25% of the numbers are greater than 0.5. If you multiply another number series, 12.5% of the numbers are greater than 0.5 and for the fourth, about 6%

of the numbers are greater than 0.5. This 6% is pretty much the percentage of new products that survive two years.

This multiplication logically corresponds to an AND link. Success is only achieved if a new product is widely distributed, has an attractive overall appearance, a reasonable price, is easily recognizable and is so good that customers want to buy it again after their first purchase.

A new type of modeling was able to discover this relationship in the data. And this despite the fact that more than 200 variables, including binary and metric variables, were available and, above all, despite the fact that nobody had expected this result in advance.

Formula 1 or off-road vehicle?

It is not the case that classic modeling methods are "bad". Quite the opposite. Within the scope of their assumptions, the methods are extremely good and extremely accurate. It's like a Formula One car. It is extremely optimized, has a high top speed and the tires can be changed in seconds.

If you order a car like this as a company car, you won't get 100 meters far. There's no trunk and no gas at the filling station. But above all, every bump on a normal road shatters the underbody into thousands of parts.

A modern AI-based analysis system is more like an off-road vehicle. It may not be as fast as a Formula 1 car. But it gets from A to B no matter what the surface looks like, whether there is a river in between or a hill to cross.

Is artificial intelligence the solution?

What is artificial intelligence and what is machine learning? The answer is quite simple: machine learning is written in Phyton and artificial intelligence in PowerPoint.

Joking aside.

Artificial intelligence originally referred to all technical systems whose behavior gives the impression of being controlled by human intelligence. For our purposes, a different definition makes more sense. This is because in many applications, AI systems are far more "intelligent" than humans in this area. This understanding of AI is particularly unhelpful in data analysis. Because what AI can achieve here is many times greater than even the most ingenious human being. What we want to do with AI is to gain insights from data and make predictions. In this context, we differentiate between statistical modeling and artificial intelligence:

> ***Statistical modeling finds the parameters of a fixed, predefined formula.***
>
> ***Artificial intelligence finds the formula itself and its parameters.***

"Machine learning" is often used as a synonym for AI, but for data scientists in particular, statistical modeling is also part of machine learning. In a sense, the machine learns by finding the parameters. This is why the majority of "AI" start-ups in Europe do not use AI at all, as a study showed a few years ago.

What exactly does the term "formula" mean in this context? Every rational explanatory approach, including a forecasting system, can be expressed as a mathematical function in which the result (the forecast) is calculated from the explanatory variables (numbers that represent certain characteristics of the causes).

The classic linear regression has this formula:

> ***Result = Variable_1 x Coefficient_1 + Variable_2 x Coefficient_2 +... + Variable_N x Coefficient_N + Constant***

The formula consists of added terms and a constant. The coefficients and the constant are calculated by the algorithm in such a way that the result of the sample data in the data set (estimated value) comes closest to the actual result.

In addition to addition, there are other basic arithmetic operations such as multiplication. The basic arithmetic operations are possible basic building blocks that can be used to construct ANY function. There are also other basic building blocks that can be used to construct arbitrary functions. A neural network uses an S-shaped function as a basic building block and with its addition you can also build any other function (the mathematician Kolmogorov proved this 100 years ago).

The following image of mountains has always helped me: The longitude and latitude represent the explanatory variables. The height of a mountain at a certain point (= combination of longitude and latitude) is the result you are looking for. There is now a mathematical function that describes every mountain (except for a neglectable deviation). The AI can find this unknown function.

All that AI glitters is not gold.

To stay with the image of the mountains. AI is like a forestry company that cuts down trees in the mountains and notes the longitude, latitude and altitude on each tree. At the sawmill, the AI can then estimate the shape of the mountain based on the data on the trees.

Okay, there are a few gaps. For example, where no trees grow. This is also the case in corporate practice. There were no major crashes in the stock market data for the last ten years (2014 - 2024). New crashes cannot be predicted from this data.

If you use a forecasting system to select and acquire target customers, this system may stop working one day. If you don't monitor the system, you will quickly go broke.

It is important to be aware of these framework conditions. Otherwise you run the risk of becoming a victim of "Black Swan" phenomena.

But there are even more serious problems.

Model Drift

When I started studying in Berlin in 1993, I was always fascinated by this Reuters terminal that stood in the middle of the canteen. The student stock exchange association had set it up there. The monitor showed the current stock market prices in real time, which were delivered by satellite (remember: there was no internet back then!).

Then one day, Germany's biggest daily newspaper ran the headline "Artificial intelligence predicts stock market". I was fascinated. Shortly afterwards, I joined the student stock exchange association and read up on how the professionals make their investment decisions. That's when I met Harun. He was also studying electrical engineering and had caught wind of the newspaper article.

Over the next few years, we met weekly to discuss the nights and program neural networks, fortified by ready-made spaghetti. Successes and setbacks alternated.

I still remember it well. We had built a system that not only learned the training data with high accuracy, but also predicted the test data with good results. This was data from a shorter time horizon with which the neural network had not yet been trained. I ran the model training for two weeks during my vacation.

But the performance on the live data was disappointing. How could that be?

It turned out that our model was suffering from a phenomenon called "model drift". Data scientists all over the world are familiar with it. And most of them still don't have a solution. They simply retrain the model more frequently, which often only masks the problem.

If I want to predict the career success of managers on the basis of shoe size, then that at first works somewhat. For well-known reasons, men climb the career ladder more often than women. And they have the bigger shoes. When shoe fashion changes and women wear long shoes, the model starts to falter. Why? Because shoe size is not the cause of professional success.

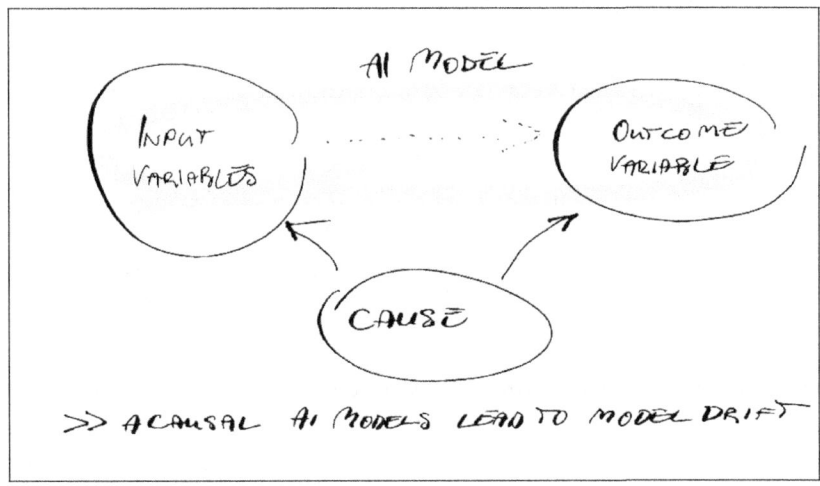

Model drift occurs when the explanatory variables/data no longer explain the target variable in the same way over time.

Discriminatory AI

Many banks use forecasting systems to predict the credit default risk of a loan applicant. There have already been several discrimination scandals in this area. What happened?

These AI systems used all available information about a customer and then tried to predict the probability of credit default from the past. However, this information is highly correlated. People with higher incomes live in different zip code areas and people with darker skin have a lower income on average.

Machine learning - AI or not - traditionally has only one goal: to reproduce the target variable as accurately as possible. If two explanatory variables are highly correlated, the algorithm does not "care" which variable is used to reproduce the result. As a result, skin color has an explanatory contribution to credit default, even if this is not (causally) justified. The causal factors are income and job security, not skin color.

It was similar with Amazon's applicant scoring models, which categorically screened out all female applicants. The learning data set was not only male-dominated. The women it contained often had less professional experience. The algorithm's only goal was to predict career success, and the gender variable was useful in identifying the "underperformers". This characteristic was not simply "politically incorrect". It was simply factually incorrect because, all other things being equal, women were just as successful.

The technical reason for the failure of classical AI and ML is that they are not designed to use only those variables that have a causal influence.

The result is not only unfair models. The result is models that deliver suboptimal or even incorrect predictions and findings in regular operation.

The main criticism of AI systems in recent years has often been their black box character. This is being worked on. Methods called "Explainable AI" have been developed. With SHARP, freely available open source libraries have been created. AI-based driver analyses have been developed, most of which use the Random Forests method and are designed to tell the user which variables have which importance.

But an a-causal random forest (or an a-causal neural network) cannot be repaired an "Explainable AI" algorithm.

Wrong remains wrong.

Explainable AI therefore offers a dangerous illusion of transparency.

Distilling alcohol in the cellar at home used to be commonplace. In some parts of the world, this is still the case today. It happened time and again that methanol was produced during distillation. The result: at best blindness, at worst instant death.

Methanol is produced by the splitting and fermentation of the pectin contained in the cell walls of the grain. If the mash is not filtered properly before distillation so that it contains hardly any cell walls, the spirit is rich in methanol.

Today, AI and machine learning are similar to the unfiltered distillation of schnapps. It often works, sometimes it goes wrong.

What we need is a filter system - also for AI.

The solution is called "CAUSAL AI"

Causal AI methods are one such "filter". They address the core of the problem: the acausal explanatory data.

The challenge posed by causal AI is a tough nut to crack. You can achieve a lot with "filter algorithms". But it turns out that a good knowledge of the real world, which is described by the data, is also very helpful here.

So what is causal AI? My simplified formula is

Causal AI = artificial intelligence + domain expertise + X

Artificial intelligence algorithms are needed to discover what is difficult or impossible for humans. To be useful for Causal AI, we place certain requirements on the AI technologies used. For example, it is not enough to map a target variable well (i.e. to obtain a good fit).

We also need the expertise and knowledge to use and process the right data. We also need it to ultimately derive definitive findings. It gives us the context that is not visible in the data itself.

We also need algorithms from time to time that check whether the conditions for causality are met. Are all important influences included in the model? What about the direction of causality? Does satisfaction influence customer loyalty or vice versa?

I will explore all of this in the next chapter. What process should we use to bring in expert knowledge? What technology should the AI algorithms use? What processes are behind the "X"? In this way, we can better understand what a good filter for AI should look like.

Key Learnings

1. *The hypothesis-based approach has its limits. It produces racing cars that are supposed to drive through open terrain.*

2. *Statistical modeling finds the parameters of a fixed, predefined formula. Artificial intelligence finds the best formula, not just the parameters.*

3. *AI suffers from model drift, discrimination and a risk of performing poorly in live operation.*

4. *Explainable AI offers a dangerous illusion of transparency.*

5. *Causal AI for AI is like the filtration system for a distillery. Ultimately, it is an absolute must.*

Chapter 3:

THE NEED

What should this mouse trap be able to do?

Three steps are required to build a powerful AI system. The creation of a comprehensive data set, the selection of a suitable machine learning algorithm and the application of certain algorithmic and human evaluation methods. Why this is the case and what needs to be taken into account will be explained now. It will be the most methodical chapter in this book, but I will try to make it interesting and understandable.

Step #1 - Collect a holistic dataset

Swiss insurance companies often take a closer look than others. I like it when customers ask "Is that possible?" questions. That's when the inventor in me comes out and starts tinkering. It was the same here.

We had just built a causal AI system that explained what drives NPS and how to strategically optimize it. In the dashboard simulator, it was possible to make improvements in certain CX topic and then see how much the insurer's NPS would improve.

But then came the question: "What good is one more NPS point anyway?" Melanie asked freely. Such questions are at the beginning of every innovation.

In our case, we decided to request a data set from the data team that would show the characteristics of the customers surveyed in the past and then also find out whether these customers had churned from their contracts in the following year.

An initial analysis made us suspicious. The NPS value correlated positively with customer churn. The more loyal the customers, the more likely they were to churn? "That can't be right," we said to ourselves and built an initial forecasting model that used the NPS rating and some information about the customer to predict whether they would churn. The influence of the NPS was now very small, but still positive.

I looked at the first model and realized that many of the available variables had not been included in the model. In particular, the internal segmentation of customers had not yet been taken into account.

Now you might ask: "What does this have to do with the influence of loyalty on churn? The answer became more than clear in this project.

The resulting model not only had a better predictive quality, it also showed a clearly negative influence of loyalty (NPS rating) on customer churn.

What had happened?

By integrating additional variables, we have taken so-called confounder effects into account. This confounder was called "customer segment".

The insurance company had a higher-value customer segment that was obviously more selective and documented this attitude with a lower rating. With the same level of loyalty, these people would be more likely to give a lower NPS rating. The causal influence of segment affiliation on the loyalty measure was negative.

At the same time, the tendency to churn was lower in this upmarket segment, as they were generally better looked after. The causal influence of segment affiliation on churn was positive.

If an external variable (segment affiliation) influences two variables at the same time, then these variables correlate for this reason. In this case, the correlation is negative, as the loyalty measure is influenced negatively and churn positively - i.e. in the opposite direction.

If this external variable - this so-called confounder - is not included in the model, the model will show a causal relationship that does not actually exist.

In science and data science practice, a procedure known as "p-value hacking" is common. The p-value stands for the significance of a correlation. In order to obtain more significant correlations in statistical models, it is helpful to remove more and more variables from the model. However, each elimination not only increases the significance of the correlations, but also the probability that the model will produce causally incorrect results.

It has taken a few decades, but now even the American Statistical Society has clarified the limitations of significance tests as a key quality criterion in a statement. But I think it will take another two or three generations before this becomes common practice.

Whenever we cannot fall back on robust theories (which is almost always the case in marketing), causal models are those that take many variables into account. They do this with the aim of reducing the risk of confounders by modeling their effects.

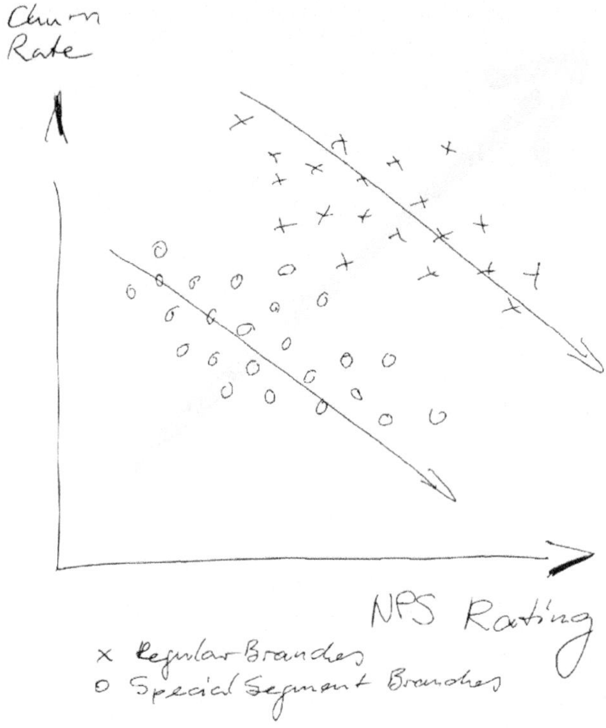
Churn Rate
NPS Rating
x Regular Branches
o Special Segment Branches

It's a bit like the hare and the hedgehog. The hedgehog crosses the finish line first and you automatically conclude that he must be faster. The fallacy, however, is the length of the path that the hedgehog has surreptitiously shortened.

Don't be fooled by the hedgehog. Don't just look at the data. You can't measure cause-and-effect relationships, you can't see them. You can only deduce them indirectly. You have to be very careful not to let the hedgehog get the better of you.

Marketing & business expertise helps with variable selection

At Success Drivers, we have been analyzing the data from Microsoft's global B2B customer satisfaction surveys for many years. I still remember the day Angelika, a project manager with us, came to see me. She had developed an AI driver analysis model that explained what drives satisfaction. In line with the guidelines, she had not only incorporated the measured partial satisfaction into the model, but also various other characteristics from the data set to make it more holistic.

She proudly said: "Frank, we now have an explanation quality of 0.88". That made me sit up and take notice. "What are the main drivers," I asked. "That's the IRO," she said?

Neither she nor I knew what this mysterious IRO was supposed to be. We checked with Microsoft and learned that particularly dissatisfied customers were flagged and then contacted. This variable was not a cause, but a consequence, which we tried to explain.

The AI model didn't care. It did what it was told: to find the function with which we could predict the result of the input variables well.

The entire model was worthless. IRO has a part of the target variable in it and thus makes the model no longer interpretable. It is therefore part of the action instruction that only driver variables that can principally be logically causal are used.

"Do you always know?" I'm often asked. Of course you don't always know. But marketing science provides a framework in which most variables in the marketing context can be categorized.

There are variables that relate to the results and status in the marketing funnel. These are, for example, the purchase intention, the consideration/evoked set and the awareness. These variables have a logical sequence. Purchase intention, for example, is a downstream stage of consideration.

The status of the marketing funnel is influenced by the perception of the product and the brand. Do consumers perceive the product as tasting good, healthy or trustworthy? These are product and brand-specific attitudes. And here, too, there are logical causalities. The brand influences the perception of the product. Of course, there is also a reverse causal effect, but this takes place on a longer-term timeline. I will discuss this shortly.

These perceptions and attitudes change as a result of experiences with the product and the brand. This can be the consumption of the product, an advertising contact, a conversation with a friend or a television report. In marketing, these experiences are often referred to as "touchpoints".

How the touchpoints in turn influence the attitude towards the product and the marketing funnel can vary depending on the target group and situation. It therefore makes sense to include characteristics of the person (e.g. demographics) and the situation (e.g. seasonality) as possible moderating variables.

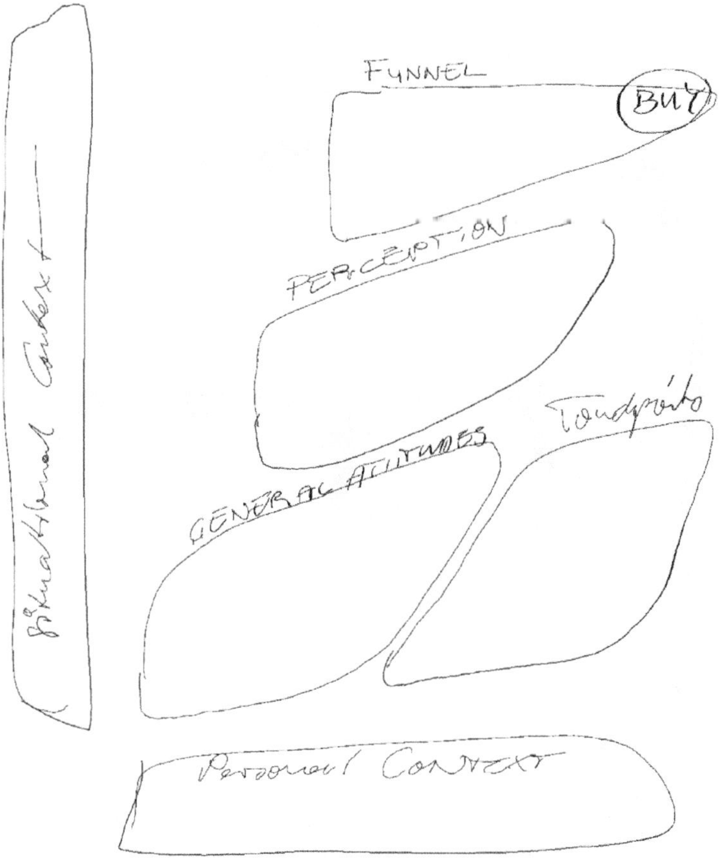
FUNNEL
BUY
PERCEPTION
GENERAL ATTITUDES
Touchpoints
Situational Context
Personal Context

There are hypotheses about what works and hypotheses about what doesn't work. According to Nassim Taleb, the latter are easier to set up. It is easier for us humans to know, for example, that overall satisfaction has no influence on service satisfaction than to know that service satisfaction has a decisive influence on overall satisfaction.

Therefore, it is not the aim of the above framework to define which variable influences which causal relationship. Rather, the aim is to specify to the model which causal relationships can be logically excluded with a high degree of probability.

To speak in images: It is relatively safe to say that a pope is a human being. However, a more intensive check is required to identify a person as a pope. We want to leave this check to the AI if we cannot do it ourselves with certainty.

You don't know what you don't know

The non-profit organization "Kindernothilfe" wanted to revise its marketing strategy and, as a first step, better understand how donors choose the non-profit organization.

At Success Drivers, we usually solve this question by designing a questionnaire that collects the data we need according to the framework mentioned above by interviewing the target customers. For example, we held a workshop with the organization to fill in the categories of the framework. This usually happens quite quickly because we find a lot of things in old questionnaires and documents that we just have to assign.

Nevertheless, it is worth investing a lot of time in brainstorming. In this project, I realized this again by a happy coincidence: at the beginning of the questionnaire, we asked the respondents which aid organization they knew. From the list of known ones, another one was selected in addition to Kindernothilfe. These two brands were then evaluated in order to be able to understand in retrospect what motivates donors to prefer an aid organization.

This question was therefore only intended as a control question. When we were building the model, we had this information in the data set about which aid organizations a respondent knew. I noticed that some respondents knew a lot of aid organizations and others only knew very few. My intuition told me that this could be a useful information in the marketing funnel. So this variable was included in the model.

In fact, it turned out that this variable plays a central role. Donors who know many providers proved to be much more selective. It is much more difficult to win them over because they have many points of comparison.

That's another insight where you say to yourself: "Yes, of course, that's logical". But nobody in the workshop had ever said that before.

Such "it's obvious" aha-experiences have been with me since I started using Causal AI for companies, and we'll talk about a few more.

The wider we cast the net, the more variables we collect about potentially influential facts, the better the causal model of reality becomes and the more astonishing the "aha" moments.

It was not only useful to realize that donors who only know a few providers are easier to win over. It turned out that younger potential donors naturally know fewer providers. "Also clear" - but unfortunately only in retrospect. In addition, people who know few providers can be found in other places and at other contact points.

In short, the entire marketing strategy has been turned on its head as young target groups suddenly come into focus.

We overestimate the relevance of what we know and underestimate the relevance of what we don't know. That is why it is so helpful to think "out of the box". It is precisely this process of taking a holistic approach that will require human experts for a while yet. At least a human, inspired by LLMs, will be able to do it. The expertise required here has nothing to do with data science.

To put it metaphorically, everyone knows the situation: You have a problem, but you can't find a solution. No matter how hard you try. Then, in the shower, the idea comes. You can't think of a word, no matter how hard you try. In a relaxed moment, it comes out of nowhere. When we concentrate too much, we focus on what we have access to (knowing) and not on what is associative further away (not knowing or early knowing). Then we miss the chance to find solutions that lie outside the current paradigm.

Most scientific breakthroughs were not made possible by a research plan, but by unplanned "coincidences". Whether Penecilin, Post-Its, airbags, microwave devices or Teflon - great inventions are the result of lucky coincidences and thinking "outside the box".

If you want to lead your company into a new phase of growth, it is helpful not only to focus on what you know, but above all to look for insights where your own knowledge is limited. This is exactly the idea of "Causal AI" - **using knowledge to explore the unknown**.

Step #2 - Choose a suitable machine learning algorithm

When I started experimenting with neural networks in the early 90s, I was full of enthusiasm. Harun and I collected stock market data. We "scraped" the stock prices that were broadcast on German television via screen text, because the Internet was not yet available. We thought about how we could best pre-process the data in order to feed it to a neural network.

Performance on test data (i.e. data sets that the system had not yet learned) was terrible. Even linear regression was better. Something was going wrong. What could it be? There were so many variables. Network architecture, learning methods, number of parameters, pre-initialization, better preprocessing, and so on. We tried out a lot. Really a lot. I learned that you can waste a lot of time if you try things out without questioning your paradigm. I learned that A/B testing has serious practical limitations. Fortunately, we were students, we had the time, and it took us a year or two to realize that all the methods, even those described so promisingly in the textbooks, are of little use if you ignore the so-called **"regularization"**.

What is that? All machine learning methods have a common goal: they try to minimize the prediction error. And this goal is precisely the problem. The prediction error naturally only relates to the data that is available for learning. However, the goal must be that the prediction based on situations that have not yet been seen (i.e. input data) has a minimal error.

This is a dilemma. I could use the test data for learning to improve the model with even more data. But in the live application, there will always be new, unseen input data. You have to accept that a model not only needs to fit better, but also needs to become generalizable. Regularization achieves this by following the philosophical principle of "Occam's razor": When in doubt, used the simpler model.

Regularization methods attempt to make a model simpler while sacrificing as little as possible of the predictive accuracy of the training data.

The figure shows the learning data as crosses. The thin line is the model that is only aimed at minimizing the prediction error. The thick line is the regularized model.

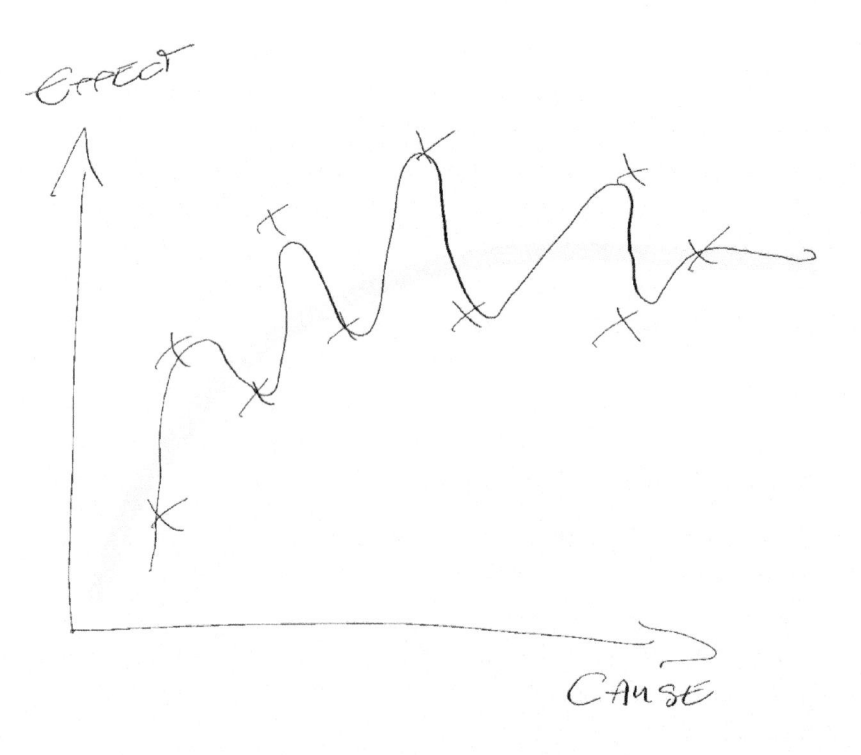

These methods form the basis of many AI systems today.

As soon as we had tried out the regularization methods in our student programming circle, the system became usable. However, the results only became really good after a further step towards causality.

Interdependencies between the causes

Marketing is one of the most complicated fields you can choose. It is often ridiculed by technical professions. They think: "They're just talking". I have to admit that I thought the same thing at the beginning of my studies. We looked down on the business economists who didn't have to and couldn't solve really complicated higher mathematics like we did.

But over the course of the semester, I realized that the natural sciences are actually comparatively simple. The math is complex but not complicated. You can experiment relatively easily and get immediate feedback. That's why we know relatively much in the natural sciences and relatively little in marketing. Marketing is like open-heart surgery, on millions of hearts at the same time.

There are so many uncontrollable variables. That's what Causal AI is all about: we want to be able to capture and understand the complexity. Then you realize that most of the variables correlate with each other. And that's a problem. Because that makes it more difficult to determine which variable is causal.

This was also the case with Kindernothilfe. The older the potential donors are, the more often and the more they donate. This is well known and leads to senior citizens being the focus of fundraising. Is this justified?

Many other variables also correlate. Various components of brand perception correlate strongly. Even wealth and income correlate.

It turns out that although classic machine learning and AI produce precise estimates for the training data, the more variables are involved, the more they have to contend with multicollinearity. As an undesirable side effect, variables are used in the model that have no direct causal influence. This in turn leads to unstable forecasts and distorted attributions of causes.

There are two algorithmic methods in particular that are used by AI systems to measure causal effects more accurately.

1. Double Machine Learning (DML)

Back to the SONOS example. When we predict loyalty from the other data using an AI model, the prediction contains all the information of the explanatory variables that the algorithm could use. What remains (the difference between prediction and actual value) is called "noise" (i.e. an unexplained random component). If the explanatory variables (=causes) do not fully explain the loyalty (=effect), *part of* the "noise" is the actual information contained in the loyalty variable.

This is also the case when we explain the "service evaluation" with an AI model. Double Machine Learning now attempts to explain the "intrinsic information" of the target variable through that of the other variables by working with adjusted variables.

The method consists of two stages of machine learning. Hence the name "Double". In the first stage, machine learning models, e.g. a neural network, are trained for each variable that is influenced by other variables. This also includes the target variable, such as loyalty.

For the second step, the difference between the predicted value of the machine learning procedure and the actual value is calculated (this difference is referred to as the residual). The second step now calculates a machine learning model **using only the residuals**, not the actual values.

It's a bit like tracking. You won't see the snow fox that only roams around at night. But its tracks in the snow can tell us where it is coming from and where it is going.

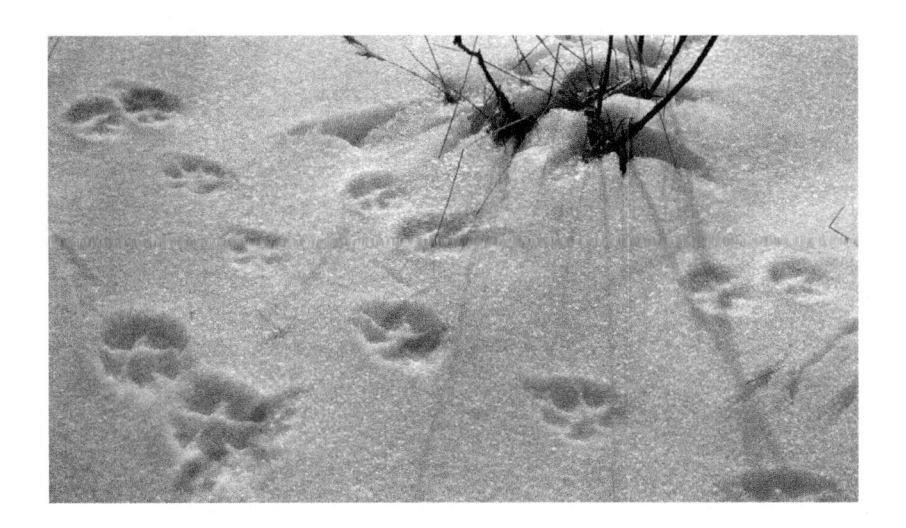

2. Automated Relevance Detection (ARD)

There is another method to get a grip on the interdependencies between the explanatory variables. The idea is to try to eliminate the explanatory variables during the AI's iterative learning process without losing accuracy, instead of using a two-stage approach.

So the idea is to integrate this goal into the AI's objective function. What does objective function mean? Neural networks are optimized by setting up a function (= formula) that expresses what you want to achieve. In the simplest case, this is the "sum of the amounts of all differences between the actual and the predicted value for each case/data set". This sum should be small.

This formula now depends on the weights (=parameters) of the neural network. The learning algorithm, in turn, is a method that knows how the weights must be iteratively changed bit by bit so that the sum of this formula becomes smaller.

Automated Relevance Detection (ARD) has changed its objective function so that the goal is not only to minimize the prediction error, but also to omit dependent variables. It's not about black or white, not about in or out, but about a trade-off. It's a balancing process. Weighing up how fit should be weighed up against the simplicity of the model. This is a learning process in itself, which is implemented by the procedure using the principles of Bayesian statistics.

It's a bit like the job of hunters. Their job is to keep the food chain in balance. How many predators does it take? How much prey? How much pasture grass? But what exactly the right balance is, is not a trivial question. The ARD algorithm investigates this question in an iterative search process.

Modern "Causal AI" has therefore typically implemented Automated Relevance Detection (ARD) and / or Double Machine Learning (DML).

Unexpected non-linearities

"Marketing works a little differently in the pharmaceutical sector," Daniel explains to me, pointing to a graphic. His company, which was part of Solvay at the time, produced prescription drugs. Marketing is mainly done through channels and campaigns designed to convince doctors to consider a drug.

Of course, there are also advertisements in specialist journals. But the majority of the budget is spent on equipping the sales force to keep doctors well informed and make a good impression. The whole thing is not called marketing, but "commercial excellence". At its core, however, it is all about the same questions: Which channels and campaigns are effective? How can I sell more?

We helped Daniel to structure the problem and then collect data. In a pilot country, all sales representatives were asked to collect data for their sales territory and the last 24 months. In addition to the target figure "number of prescriptions", we compiled the most important measures. These included the number of visits, participation in workshops, invitations to conferences, the distribution of brand reminders such as pens, product samples and much more. We collected 480 data records from over 20 sales territories, which enabled us to analyze the data across 14 channels.

We applied our Causal AI software and once again the results were surprising: it was to be expected that the number of sales visits was an important driver. But the overall impact of product samples was zero. "Product samples are important," I remembered Daniel saying.

I looked at the plots of the non-linear relationships. It looked strange. The plots showed the result of a simulation: how many additional prescriptions can be expected if the number of product samples per doctor is increased or reduced to a certain value.

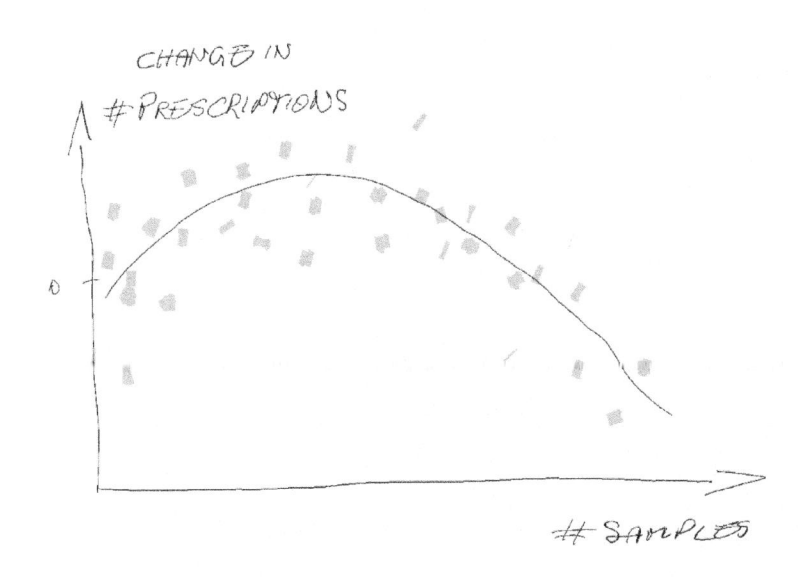

[Hand-drawn graph: inverted U-curve with scatter points. Y-axis labeled "CHANGE IN # PRESCRIPTIONS" with 0 marked. X-axis labeled "# SAMPLES".]

The graph shows an inverted U-function. There was a value for the number of product samples at which the effect was maximum. It took a while for it to click. "That's logical," I thought to myself. If the sales force distributes too many product samples, at some point the doctors will no longer have enough patients to prescribe the medicine to. Instead, the product samples are then handed out instead of prescriptions. The product samples then replace the prescriptions instead of promoting them.

The software found something that we hadn't thought of before. In hindsight, it was as clear as day.

This example is intended to show one thing: Reality is often different than we think. It is also usually more complex than we think, because we humans are used to thinking one-dimensionally and linearly. Because this is the case, we need causal AI methods that can detect unknown non-linearities without having to specify them with hypotheses beforehand.

It's a bit like a small child playing a pegging game. It can be so frustrating when the cube doesn't fit into the round hole. No amount of kicking or hammering will help. A causal AI, like the one we need, first looks to see what kind of hole we have and can then put the right object into it.

Unexpected interactions

Remember the Mintel case study above? Here, Causal AI has discovered interaction effects that we didn't have on screen before.

Interactions are similar to non-linearities. Unfortunately, many managers do not intuitively understand what exactly is meant by the term "interaction" in methodological terms. So here is a definition:

Interaction or moderation effect:

We speak of interaction or moderation when the extent or manner in which a causal variable acts depends on another causal variable.

In this case, two (or more) variables "interact" in their effect. The degree of distribution "only promotes sales" if the product looks attractive, and it is only bought again if it tastes good. The effect of each component depends on the strength of the others.

Interaction effects are different from mediation effects:

Intermediation or mediation effect:

Conversationally, the term interaction is often used when one causal variable (e.g. friendliness) influences another causal variable (e.g. service quality) and this in turn influences the result (e.g. loyalty). However, this must be distinguished from a genuine interaction. That is why we have a different term for it: (inter)mediation. In this example, the mediator is the service quality.

To find interactions, we again need a machine learning approach that is flexible enough to see and find what is there. Many causal AI approaches, on the other hand, work on the basis of so-called "structural equations" or "causal graphs". Here, the analyst determines which variable may have an effect on which variable. However, this unconsciously makes a fatal assumption: the assumption that the effects of the variables add up. Each interaction is considered individually and its effect should add up. Unknown interactions are thus excluded.

Step #3 - Simulate, Test, Repeat

In Step#1, I described how important it is to create a holistic data set and to have the knowledge about the real-world topic that the data describes. In Step#2, I described what AI should be able to do to build causal models.

Now, in step 3, it's about how we should use these AI models to derive causally useful knowledge.

Illuminating the black box

The AI finds the formula hidden in the data. As such, it follows the flexible structural logic of a neural network and does not fit directly into the framework of human thinking.

Human thinking consists of logical connections based on categorizations (black and white). Continuous connections can only be understood as "the more - the better/worse". The requirement to make the findings of AI understandable for humans is the requirement to simplify the findings and translate them into the structure of human language.

A neural network does not tell us how important the input variables are, nor how they are related. The weights in neural networks have no fixed meaning and this is only formed in the context of all the other weights. The first hidden neuron is interchangeable with the second. The position plays no role. Only the result of all neurons together has a meaning. In this respect, an analysis of the weights is only of limited use.

What you can do is to research the properties of the unknown function by simulation.

Let's stay with Daniel and his Pharma Commercial Excellence success model and run some simulations together with the variable "number of product samples".

Average Simulated Effect (ASE): For each data set we have (a sales territory in a given month), we simply increase the number of product samples by 1 and then see how many prescriptions the neural network predicts as a result. If providing product samples works, the average number of prescriptions should increase. This was not the case with Daniel. The average simulated effect was close to zero. So did the variable have no effect?

No. To understand this, we carry out these further simulations:

Overall Explain Absolute Deviation (OEAD): To do this, we manipulate the "product sample" variable again. This time we replace the actual data of this variable with a constant value. To do this, we take the average number of product samples. The output of the neural network now provides different values. The predicted values resulting from the real data are close to the actual prescription numbers (small error). The forecast values resulting from the manipulated data are no longer as accurate. They have a larger error. By measuring how much explanation we lose for prescribing behavior when we no longer have the information from the "product samples" variable, we can measure the importance of the variables to us. In Daniel's case, this value was quite high. So it was an important variable. But there was no simple explanatory (monotonic) relationship.

But how does this relationship look like?

Non-linear curves: All we have to do is look at the individual values of the OEAD simulation in a diagram. The diagram shows the number of product samples on the horizontal axis (X). We create a point in the diagram for each data set. On the vertical axis (Y), we plot the CHANGE that results for this data set in the target variable (number of prescriptions) if we replace the value of the number of product samples with its mean value.

What we now see in Daniel's example is a U-shaped relationship. The points do not form a clear line, but a cloud of points, but there is a recognizable relationship. The point cloud is not created by the estimation error of the neural network, because we subtract two forecast values from the neural network and thus the random component is subtracted to zero. The point cloud is created by interactions with other variables (and model inaccuracies, which then appear as interactions).

Interaction plots: We can proceed in a similar way to visualize interaction effects. We simply take the OEAD model manipulated above and set a second variable that could interact constant. In this case, we take the number of sales visits. Again, we can visualize the result in a 3D diagram in a similar way. The horizontal dimensions are the number of product samples and the number of sales visits. The vertical dimension is again the CHANGE that results when the mean value is replaced. If the change due to the product samples is greater than the change due to the number of sales visits, we have an interaction. This then becomes visually apparent. This can then be recorded again in a key figure.

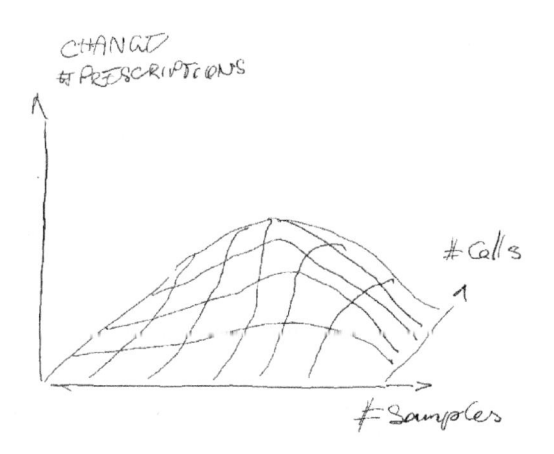

Metaphorically speaking, these simulations work like the human eye. In reality, the human eye only sees a small section. It sees the section that it focuses on. It sees what is by moving the eye minimally. The difference allows us to understand what is and to filter out the insignificant. If our muscles, including the eye muscles, were paralyzed, we would no longer see anything. So these simulations are like our eyes, allowing us to see a complex world.

All these simulations can be converted into key figures. With the help of bootstrapping, we can also calculate significance values for these correlations. The procedure is very simple. From a sample of N data records, N data records are drawn at random (with "putting them back" procedure). This means that some data records may occur twice, others not at all. In this way, a bootstrap data set is created. It represents a possible alternative data set that could be drawn in a similar way the next time. You now draw dozens or, if possible, hundreds of these bootstrap data sets. Different KPIs are obtained for each of these data sets, such as ASE. If these values are close to each other, the significance is high.

But be careful. "Significant" does not mean "important" or "relevant". It only means "an effect is present provided that the model is meaningful". Since many users (even in science) do not understand the true meaning of significance, significance hacking is practiced in science and practice. The smaller (and therefore more unrealistic) a model becomes, the higher the significance value. In this way, variables that do not fit the picture are filtered out just to give the appearance of quality.

In fact, "significance" is largely irrelevant to business practice. Even the American Association of Statistical Science recently confirmed my personal findings from practice in a 6-point statement.

What we want to know in practice is whether a cause is "relevant". The OEAD above measures such relevance and is a kind of measure of effect size. In Bayesian statistics, there is the concept of evidence. A correlation is evident if it is statistically relevant and the model makes sense (in accordance with the wisdom of the field). A small, overly simple model makes little sense and can therefore only provide limited evidence, even if we can demonstrate an effect size. In STEP #1 above we ensure meaningfulness, in STEP #2 we model the actual effects and in STEP #3 we measure their RELEVANCE.

To illustrate this, let's look at weightlifters and bodybuilders. It is highly significant that bodybuilders are strong and powerful. But this strength is not relevant. It would be relevant if you could lift particularly heavy weights with it, for example. But bodybuilders would lose every competition in all weightlifting competitions. The picture shows what the record holder in weightlifting looks like. Actually, the bodybuilder would be expected to do much more, but that's just for show. Just like the significance values, are for the „show" only.

Deriving total effects

We stick with Daniel and his model to explain the prescription figures. Each time the sales force visited a physician, product samples, brand reminders and new information material were distributed. There were times when no product samples were distributed. Typically, however, it was customary to distribute some samples.

Methodologically, this habit is reflected in an indirect causal effect. This is because when the sales managers increased the frequency of their visits, they also increased the number of samples handed out in line with the usual and expected ritual. The effect was also reversed. Consequently, the two variables correlated strongly with each other.

In order to determine the overall effect of the distribution visits, both the direct effect (= the effect of the visits) and the indirect effect (= the effect of the samples multiplied by the probability of issuing samples during a visit) must be taken into account. This indirect effect arises from the fact that more visits also result in more samples being distributed. This is because management only asks one question: "What happens if I change cause X?"

The total ASE is the direct ASE plus the indirect ASE. The indirect ASE is the ASE on the number of samples multiplied by the ASE on the number of samples multiplied by the number of prescriptions.

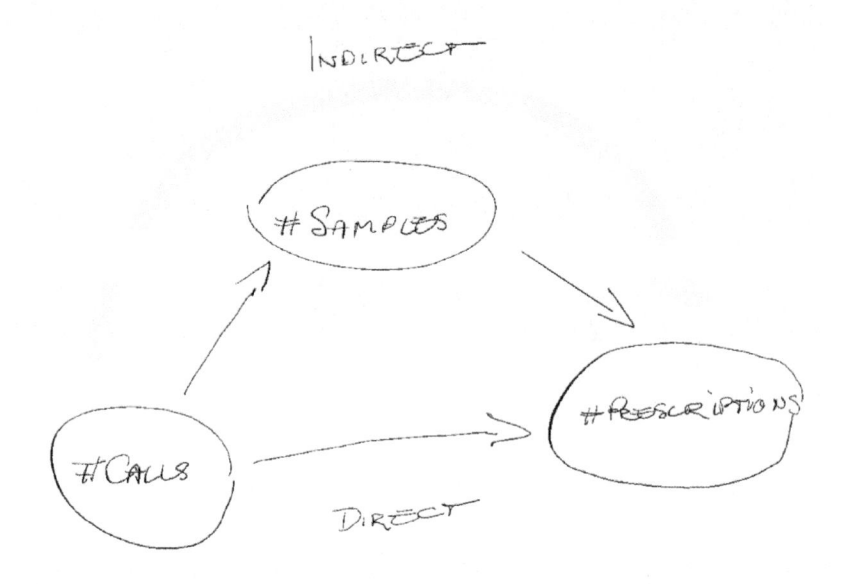

INDIRECT

 # SAMPLES

 # CALLS → *# PRESCRIPTIONS*

DIRECT

The total OEAD can be calculated in the same way. Of course, there are many indirect effects in complex cause-and-effect networks, some of which are interlinked or even circular. However, all these effects can be calculated with the help of software and combined to form an overall effect.

The Total OEAD tells me whether a variable is relevant. The Total ASE tells me how large the (monotonic) effect of an incremental increase in a cause is on average.

Orchestra musicians know this best. The room, the orchestra hall, is crucial for the sound. Only some of the sound waves reach the listener's ear directly. There are many indirect reflections, which then make up the fullness of the sound. The sound measurements on the instruments symbolize the action variables, the measurements on the walls of the hall the intermediate variables and the coughing of the person sitting next to you the situational variables.

It is clear that the impact of an action can only be properly measured if the indirect paths are not taken into account.

Checking the causal direction

When we implemented the first algorithms for causal direction detection in our NEUSREL software in 2012, we came across some astonishing results. The first use case was data from the American Satisfaction Index. In the structural equation model used in marketing, satisfaction influences loyalty and not the other way around. Satisfaction is a short-term changing opinion about a brand. Loyalty, on the other hand, is an attitude that only changes in the long term. Marketing science has discovered this.

However, our algorithms revealed a clear, different picture. Loyalty influences satisfaction. Not the other way around! Was everything really okay with the algorithms?

Then it clicked: Both were right! Only in its own way.

The data are responses from consumers in a survey. If someone is loyal but dissatisfied, they tend to indicate a higher level of satisfaction than they actually feel because of their loyalty. This is a kind of psychological response bias. In this sense, current loyalty has a causal influence on current reported satisfaction.

Things look different with a different time horizon. If the same people were surveyed again with a time lag, it would be found that a low level of satisfaction - over a certain period of time - leads to a drop in loyalty.

Ergo. Causality is always linked to a time horizon. Understanding and demonstrating this is also the task of marketing managers. A purely data-driven view is blind here.

Another example? If you wade barefoot through the cold November rain, you risk catching a cold. The cold doesn't make you ill. But it weakens the immune system. If there is a virus in the body, the likelihood of an outbreak increases.

Conversely, if you regularly expose yourself to the cold, you strengthen your immune system, boost the performance of your mitochondria and are less susceptible to colds in the long term. Walking barefoot leads to fewer colds in the long term, not more colds.

There are many such examples. If you wash your hair often, you will have well-groomed, grease-free hair. If you don't wash your hair, you will soon notice, because your hair quickly becomes greasy. However, if you never wash your hair, your hair roots will not become greasy anymore in the long term because your hair already has a small, healthy greasy film. The hair will also look healthy and well-groomed (if you comb it).

It can therefore be seen that the topic of causality requires human supervision. First of all, we have to define for ourselves which horizon of effect we are interested in.

In addition, most causal directions in marketing can be derived from common sense and specialist knowledge. For the remaining relationships , test procedures can be used to learn. I would like to discuss the two most commonly used concepts here: The PC algorithm and the Additive Noise Model.

The PC algorithm

The PC algorithm (named after Peter Spirtes and Clark Glymour) is a machine learning method that is used to determine the structure of causal networks in data. The algorithm attempts to discover causal relationships between variables by analyzing so-called "conditional independencies" in the data.

The figure shows how the algorithm extracts pairs of three and uses the "conditional dependencies" (black arrows) to triangulate which causal directions logically result from this. If A correlates with C and

B correlates with C, but A does not correlate with B, then it follows that A and B have an effect on C and not vice versa. If this were not the case, A and B would have to correlate.

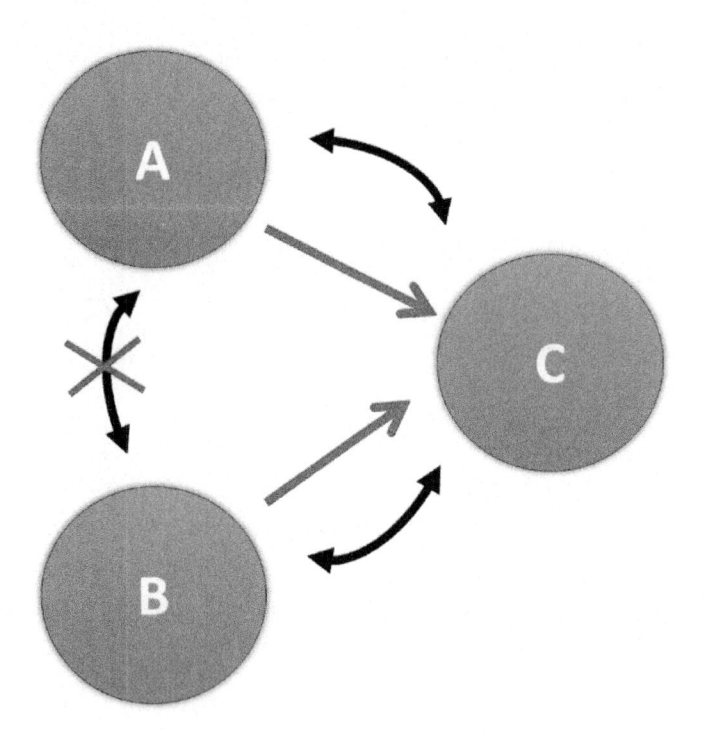

The method focuses on linear relationships, but can be extended to non-linear relationships. However, studies show that the rate of incorrect decisions increases rapidly with the size of the causal network. It is therefore recommended to use this method only for small models with less than 20 variables. The example above is an extreme example. In reality, we are dealing less with black and white and more with shades of gray. It is therefore becoming increasingly difficult to clearly prove the causal directions when effect sizes of a path (edge) is low.

Additive Noise Modeling

Additive noise modeling is a method to find out whether something (let's call it A) causes something else (B) or vice versa. It is based on the idea that if A causes B, the change in B cannot be explained by A alone, but that there is also some "noise" (unforeseen influences or chance) that is added. Importantly, this noise has nothing to do with A.

The figure below shows the same data on the left and right, except that the variable X is plotted once horizontally and once vertically. A simple linear regression is shown by the red line. The fit (or the error) of the regression (coefficient of determination R2) is exactly the same in both cases. However, the deviation (the extent of the scatter) of the regression is constant in the left-hand case and not in the right-hand case. Assuming independent noise, X must be the cause of Y and not vice versa.

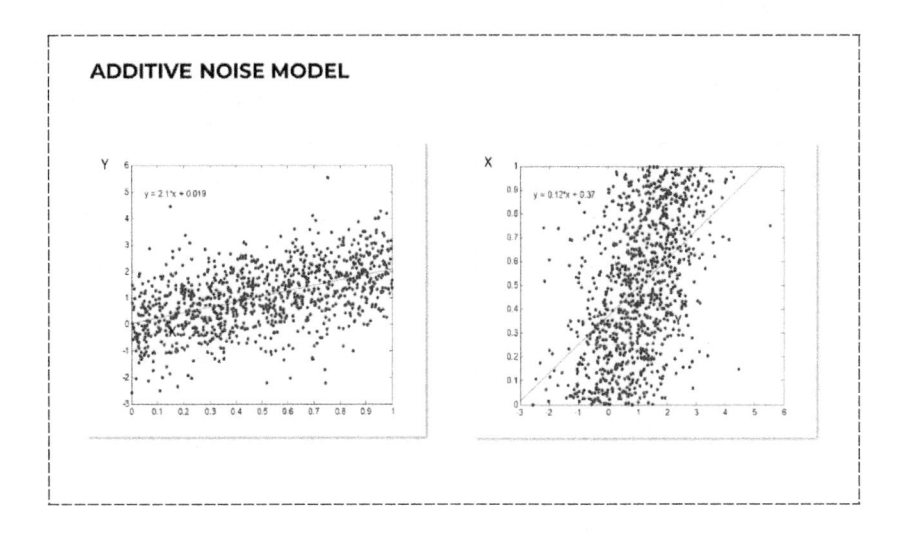

To decide whether A causes B or B causes A, we look at both possibilities and try to determine in which situation the noise is truly independent of its assumed cause. If it appears that the noise is only independent if we assume that A causes B (and not the other way around), then we would say that it is likely that A actually causes B.

The method is based on the assumption that the noise is truly independent and that the relationship between A and B is adequately captured by the model. If this is not the case, the method can lead to incorrect conclusions. Therefore, modeling that is as close to reality as possible is an important prerequisite for this test.

It's a bit like trying to work out which way is up and which way is down, assuming that the gravitational force is coming from the earth. If you turn your head, your hair should hang down.

To summarize, there are several methods for testing the direction of causality. None of them offers a silver bullet. Therefore, a conscious approach and the inclusion of expert knowledge is essential.

Check whether confounders are at work

A telecommunications company asked us to forecast the risk of customer churn. The company had already implemented a number of customer retention measures and wanted to know how well they were working. The focus of interest was the so-called "cuddle calls". Here, customers were called as a precaution to ask them about their satisfaction, simply to show appreciation and, if necessary, to hear whether someone was at risk of churning.

The figures were shocking: households that had accepted a cuddle call had twice as high a cancellation rate the following year as households that had not accepted a cuddle call. The program was on the cancelation list. It was suspected that customers at risk of churning (so-called "sleepers") were being activated by these calls.

Our first churn model also seemed to confirm this. The flag variable "cuddle call" had a positive influence on the probability of termination.

We then enriched the data with sociographic data and expanded the modeling. The result: cuddle calls now reduce the probability of quitting! How did this happen?

We had introduced a confounder into the model. It turned out that most households cannot be reached by phone during the day and that this accessibility represents a strong filter for making calls. Socially disadvantaged households in particular were reachable and these had a significantly higher probability of termination per se.

The cuddle call correlates positively with the probability of quitting, because target groups with an affinity for quitting were easier to reach by phone - not because the call was ineffective - on the contrary.

It really is like a puppet show. As children, we see how the puppets move. The robber hits the farmer and he falls down. Only apparently. In reality, there is a cause that we don't see: the puppeteer.

It is the same with the data. If we do not see the puppeteer (we have no data about him in the model), then we infer false cause-effect relationships from correlations.

So how can we check whether disturbance variables influence our model? We use two methods in the NEUSREL software:

The Hausman Test

This test has similarities with additive noise modeling and also with double machine learning. Its thesis: If the residuals, the so-called noise of the target variable (i.e. the difference between the prediction and the actual value), can be explained by the causes themselves, then they are not causes. So if the explanatory variables are used to predict the residuals with the help of an AI model, then this is an indicator of confounders.

After the Hausman test, the same modeling is carried out again - only with the residuals as the target variable. The same AI algorithms are used and the same simulation algorithms are used to calculate the effect size OEAD in particular.

So if you have clear indications as to whether a confounder is at work, you can do some soul-searching and sometimes it becomes clear which data sources you may have forgotten to use.

However, if no other data can be obtained for practical reasons, the question arises as to whether there is any way of avoiding the confounder.

Confounder elimination

In 2011 to 2013, I worked on this topic with Dr. Dominik Janzen (then Max Planck Institute, now Amazon Research) and together we came up with an idea.

If you plot the data of two (or more) explanatory variables on a two-dimensional graph, you obtain a random distribution of some kind, e.g. a Gaussian distribution. This distribution can be elongated if the variables are correlated with each other. Or it can be curved if there is a non-linear correlation.

However, if two (or more) distributions occur, i.e. if the data merge into clusters, then there must be a cause for this. This unknown cause is the confounder. It is the influence of this confounder that splits a previously uniform distribution. The information of the confounder is the vector between the clusters. This vector consists of the differences between the cluster centers.

Our procedure for "confounder elimination" now proceeds as follows

1. Search for clusters and calculate the vectors between the clusters
2. Projection of all data onto these vectors by vector multiplication
3. Use of the result as an additional variable in the AI model
4. Recalculation of the AI model.

Metaphorically speaking, confounders are like an Italian mom who distributes the spaghetti on the plates. If we follow the plates, we can understand that they have been filled by the mom and are not filling each other.

Repeat: Adjust the model on the basis of new findings

In the first step, we collected and processed data and developed a modeling approach based on existing knowledge and insights. In the second step, we causally modeled each influenced variable using a suitable AI method. In the third step, we opened the black box and conducted some tests. We will learn from the analysis of these results.

We may find that we have made a mistake. Wrong in some assumptions or wrong in the treatment of a variable. Then refinement, optimization and re-modeling is usually required.

The benchmark for optimization is not just the key metrics for model fit, causal direction or confounders. Ultimately, it is the human being who decides whether the model is meaningful and useful. This requires good specialist knowledge, wisdom and a solid foundation in causal machine learning.

What if you don't have the confidence?

Of course you can get help from external experts, but there is a second strategy: **standardization**.

Let's assume you are building a marketing mix modeling. If you have gone through the process cleanly, you can try to define all the steps in a standard. If you prepare the same type of data in the same way, model and simulate it with the same AI methods, then the results will be interpretable in the same way. If this is the case, this interpretation and consulting service can be cast in software. The entire process can then be repeated for other business units, countries or at other times with little effort.

In my view, the future for 80% of marketing issues lies in the development of standardized Causal AI-based solutions.

The term standardization is often equated with "loss of individuality" and thus loss of quality. However, this view is very short-sighted and one-eyed. A good standard process is congealed wisdom. It also ensures quality because it avoids errors. Individualization is always possible, but is associated with considerable costs.

Key Learnings

1. *Start with a blank sheet of paper and collect everything that could influence your target variable. Then collect the data.*
2. *Model the data with an AI algorithm that ensures in the learning process that forecasts are only based on causal variables.*
3. *Open the AI black box with suitable simulation algorithms.*
4. *Algorithmically check the causal directions and search for confounders.*
5. *Optimize your model and recalculate until it makes sense and is useful enough.*
6. *Standardize everything in one process - from the data, the preparation, the method to the preparation of the results.*

Chapter 4

THE VALUE

Applications of Causal AI in marketing

Theory is patient. Not every better method has to be implemented immediately. That's why it's worth taking a look at where Causal AI can be used and what practical added value it brings.

I will touch on a few fields of application as examples. You may get the impression that Causal AI is really universally applicable. You may think: "Yes, of course, that just makes more sense". This realization alone will inspire you.

Just as the benefits of mantras such as "lying doesn't pay" or "humanity wins" are not obvious in the short term, life experience shows that they work. Just as human character with integrity "pays off", more logically consistent approaches are also more successful in the long term.

So what can you do with Causal AI? I distinguish between three activities:

1. explain: Explain what causes success.

2. decide: choose automatically the best marketing actions

3. generate: create marketing content that is more effective.

It is possible to pursue several activities with one model. However, differentiating between goals leads to greater clarity of thought.

EXPLAIN better with Causal AI

Artificial intelligence has been used from the outset to automate decisions. Which product should be offered to the customer now? Which customer should be sent a mailing to discourage them from canceling? Will this customer be able to repay their loan?

For these questions, it is not necessarily problematic that AI is a black box. After all, the most important thing is to make the right decision, not to understand how it arrives at it.

But if we want to optimize the marketing mix, if we want to decide which initiatives we can use to improve the customer experience, then we need to explain what drives success. If we want to understand how we can improve our products so that they sell like hot cakes, if we want to fundamentally uncover the hidden reasons and relationships that lead to customers buying or not buying, then we should ask "why".

Today, this "why" question is answered primarily through qualitative market research and the qualitative exchange between experts. Statistical modeling is also used occasionally, but only in borderline areas due to its limitations. Each method has its value and its place. But causal AI can now cover an area that neither qualitative research nor statistical modeling could serve well.

Marketing Mix Modeling

The situation of a gambling provider was tense. Turnover had been falling for years and the managing director rightly wondered whether the millions spent on advertising had been well invested.

The advertising channels in the lottery business include traditional media such as print, posters and radio, as well as shopping radio in supermarkets and advertising at the point of sale and on websites. The media planners determine the distribution of advertising according to general principles.

Radio advertising, for example, has the fastest impact. This is why it is used massively for short-term topics such as jackpots in order to increase sales. However, these beliefs do not say exactly how much advertising pressure is needed.

Our team differentiated the use of media according to the content of the advertising. Was a jackpot advertised, was it brand advertising or a special promotion? Other important influencing factors were the size of the jackpot, the current media coverage, the specific days of the week and the time of the month.

It is always important to include all influencing variables in a model, regardless of whether they are controllable or not. This is because false results (Keyword: confounders) can only be avoided if the model is as complete as possible. If, for example, radio advertising is mainly placed on weekdays, but sales during the week are generally lower than at weekends, a negative effect would be wrongly attributed to radio. For this reason, a careful survey of possible success variables plays a central role.

The result of the analysis was surprising. Non-classical media were many times more effective than classical media. Many media channels interacted strongly with each other, so that a combined use was recommended. It was also surprising that short-term media such as radio did not have a short-term effect, but had to be used for as long as possible. However, this only seems to contradict the credo. The analysis shows that radio only creates cognitive awareness. To buy a lottery ticket, the customer must first go to the sales outlet. Hardly anyone does this just to buy a lottery ticket. As a rule, buying a lottery ticket is an impulse purchase that is merely facilitated by the awareness that has been built up beforehand. It is therefore the movement habits of the target customers that determine how quickly the advertising effect occurs and not the short-term effect of the radio.

Effekte der Kanäle

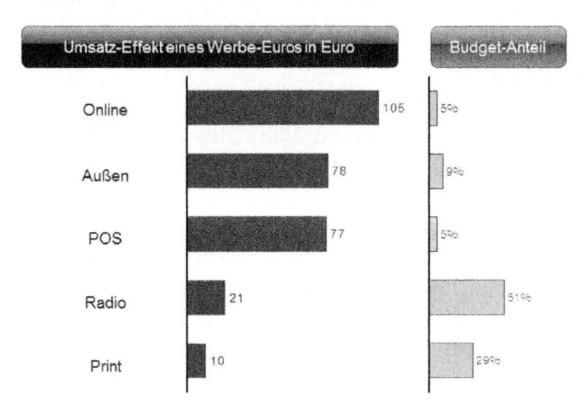

Kanal	Umsatz-Effekt eines Werbe-Euros in Euro	Budget-Anteil
Online	105	5%
Außen	78	9%
POS	77	5%
Radio	21	51%
Print	10	29%

As a result, it was shown that advertising for these gambling products is so profitable that a reallocation of the budget leads to considerable increases in efficiency. The optimization of the media plan led to continuous growth again in the following years.

In addition, the causal analysis approach provided further strategic insights. The size of the jackpot was seen as a central lever for promoting the lottery business, as the correlation between jackpot size and sales was clear. However, communication focused on jackpots leads (causally) to a drop in sales **after** the jackpot peak. Customers learn that it is not worth buying a ticket without a high jackpot. Thus, the communicative focus on the jackpot leads to the destruction of what lotto is all about - a beloved weekly habit.

So what is the difference to classic marketing mix modeling - a discipline that has been practiced for over 100 years (Unilever built its first MMM model in 1919)?

If there is one area where statistical modeling is mature, it is MMM. A lot of empirical knowledge and intuition is used to bend the models so that they "somehow" fit.

An MMM with causal AI naturally offers these advantages in particular:

- Avoidance of incorrect assignments due to non-integrated (or incorrectly integrated) confounders. One example of this is seasonal information, which is always included as a variable in a causal AI model
- Recognizes non-linear effects (e.g. saturation effects) without having to specify them in advance and recognizes interaction effects (e.g. mutual reinforcement of radio and POS advertising). The classic consideration of such hypotheses would involve extreme effort.
- Natural modeling of short, medium and long-term effects. The vast majority of advertising effects are long-term because they continue to have a long-term effect through the formation of mental structures. Ignoring this leads to misdirection in marketing.
- Avoidance of misclassification due to strongly correlated variables. Online channels in particular (earned and owned media) correlate very strongly with paid media. Here we see strong distortions in conventional mix modeling.

Customer Experience

What makes customers happy? What annoys them? How can you retain them? These are questions that an entire industry is now dealing with.

Customer satisfaction surveys have been around for a long time. However, the NPS concept has introduced a very simple methodology. Its advantage: all you need to do is ask a question at each touchpoint and, if necessary, receive an open answer. Today, CX software providers such as Qualtrics, Medallia and InMoment support the conception, implementation and evaluation. However, success is sparse and CX experts argue about why this is the case.

In my experience, one of the main reasons for this is that customer feedback is analyzed too superficially, resulting in crucial mistakes being made.

The streaming speaker brand SONOS decided to have its touchpoint surveys analyzed with Causal AI. The NPS had been declining for some time. This was explained by the fact that with increasing market penetration, other, less enthusiastic customer types were changing the customer mix. However, they were not sure.

Using Natural Language Processing, we analyzed the open responses from customers and assigned each topic that they mentioned to one of 80 categories. Tens of thousands of responses can thus be categorized with maximum precision. Today, the accuracy is even higher than when categorized by a human being. This is because humans get tired and tend to deviate from their own definitions depending on their mood.

This type of AI application in the CX area is now standard, even if many providers still use very rough, unspecific text AI models.

A look at the frequencies paints a seemingly clear picture. Almost every second customer justifies their rating with the good sound of the speakers. Unsurprisingly, there is a consensus within the company that sound quality is the key factor for customer satisfaction and customer loyalty.

Many other companies I have met are subject to the same misconception. Restaurant chains think "tastes good" is crucial, washing machine manufacturers think "washes well" and insurance companies think "has good service" are the decisive factors.

Using the categorization data, we created a causal AI model and the result was that sound quality was "nothing more" than a hygiene factor. What really engages customers is the experience of the device working properly. This could be disrupted for various technical reasons. However, this experience of smooth operation was not mentioned so often. No wonder, as there was potential for improvement.

The following graphic provides an insight into the Key Driver Matrix, which shows the frequency of naming on the vertical axis and the significance on the horizontal axis (positive on the right, negative on the left).

The tool's impact simulator can be seen on the right. Improving the software architecture for smooth operation promises an increase in NPS of 4 points. Based on the reference values determined by the modeling, these 4 points can now be converted into additional sales.

Key Drivers Matrix   **Impact Simulator**

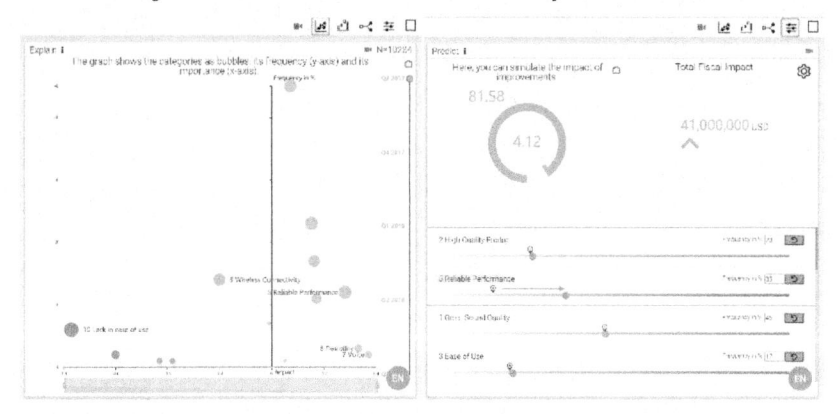

The analysis provides many other valuable insights that would have remained hidden by conventional means. For example:

- "Great Sound" is an emotional, not a technical statement: an AI score is integrated into the model that measures the tonality/emotionality of speech. According to the model, this variable "Great Sound" has an indirect effect via this emotionality. In terms of content, this means that by "Great Sound", customers mean the good feeling that the music brings and not the technical sound characteristics that the traditional hi-fi industry has always focused on.
- The product itself is very emotional. 30% of the variance is not explained by what is said, but how (with what emotionality) it is said. In comparison, this is only around 10% for insurance.
- Some topics are hygiene factors such as "ease of use" and others are excitement factors such as the "voice assistant" feature.

The topic of customer experience is a useful introduction to the topic of Causal AI. As a rule, companies are sitting on a lot of data that just needs to be analyzed in a more meaningful way. In my books "The CX

Insights Manifesto" and "CX Insights Playbook", I describe in detail how this can be achieved.

One of the advantages of using causal AI in the area of customer experience is that

- Different data sources such as binary categorization of open-ended responses can be integrated into a model with metric emotion scores and possibly Likert scales (problematic for statistical modeling).
- Indirect effects are taken into account. Topics in open-ended responses often have a different level of abstraction. For example, friendliness and good service are not causally independent. Rather, friendliness leads to good service. Taking these interdependencies into account makes it possible to better measure the causal effects and thus derive the right decisions.

Product & Innovation

Which product features are important to customers? What should be considered when developing new products? Which product features should product communication focus on? These are the classic questions that arise in the product innovation process. Interestingly, they also crop up again and again during the life cycle of the finished product, because the consumer changes and the competition changes with it.

For such questions, we at Success Drivers have created the Supra.tools platform, in which modern standardized solutions for price and product optimization as well as brand and touchpoint optimization are available. All of these solutions use causal AI. In addition, they use an innovative market research method developed in the field of neuroscience. The "Implicit Association Test" measures the unconscious opinions of consumers in a very simple way using a reaction time-based query. It is precisely this information that is decisive for purchasing decisions.

The price and product optimization of the APPLE VISION PRO was one of the first application examples that we carried out a year before the market launch. All that was needed to create the study was a product image and a description that briefly described all the relevant features in the brand's language. The tool suggests a price range and product features on an LLM basis. The latter were then verified by experts.

Subsequently, 250 computer users in the USA were surveyed, half of whom were so-called early adopters. These are people who are generally the first to buy innovative products without waiting for the product experiences of others. The willingness to pay was initially measured implicitly and the extent to which the product can actually fulfill the function of the twelve features was also implicitly queried. Features included "long battery life", "ultra high display resolution" and "easy intuitive gesture user interface".

The result was a profit-maximizing price of USD 1,999 for all consumers and USD 3,499 for early adopters. The price-profit function results from multiplying the calculated price-sales function by the price, minus the trade margin and the estimated unit costs.

Causal AI was used to determine the leverage effect of features on the willingness to buy (which the price test measures). Features that have a high leverage, but are not perceived as given or even doubted, should be improved communicatively or technically.

The following illustration shows the dashboard of the tool. The revolutionary gesture-based user guidance and the 3D applications in particular had a huge impact on the willingness to buy. At the same time, however, there was clear skepticism as to whether the user guidance would really work so intuitively.

At the launch, Apple communicated precisely these aspects and showed in videos how the user guidance works and familiar people in their usage situation.

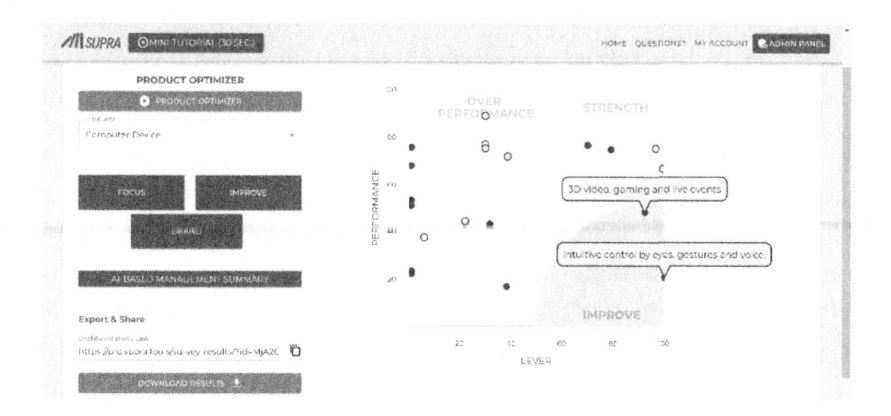

Since then, the methodology has been successfully transferred to other markets in many cases. For example, a major shoe brand has recognized that despite all the interesting features that product development has given its shoe variants, the main reason to buy a shoe is a completely different one: the design must match the customer's own style. The customer simply has to like the shoe. That sounds banal. But sometimes it is precisely this banal evidence that experts need in order to see the wood for the trees.

In traditional market research projects, conjoint measurement or MaxDiff are primarily used for such questions. The use of Causal AI combined with neuroscientific measurement methods offers the following advantages:

- 50 or more product features can be evaluated instead of a maximum of seven with conjoint measurement

- The product can be experienced in its entirety with a picture and detailed product description instead of as a bullet point list of a maximum of seven properties, as is the case with conjoint.
- The significance of the properties is derived from an implicitly measured and calibrated absolute willingness to buy instead of only in relation to a competitive set that does not exist in reality in this form and can largely change depending on the context.

An alternative is the MaxDiff method. It forces the respondent to choose between properties. It is an intelligent form of direct questioning to find out which attributes are important. As it asks directly about importance, this method is rationally biased and blind to unconscious association processes that are crucial for purchasing decisions. The new method (Supra Product Optimizer) takes both approaches into account - implicit and explicit.

Ultimately, the most important thing is the validity of the method. Is what the method determines correct? This is exactly what Causal AI is designed for - the causal attribution, the justification of what caused the purchase.

Communication & Advertising

What makes good advertising? What should advertisers pay attention to so that advertising works? What guidelines and rules of thumb help to avoid the risk of an advertising flop?

Questions that have long been left to qualitative research. However, advertising test procedures have always shown that there is an enormous discrepancy. Most commercials still today are only moderately effective, only a few are enormously effective. However, the unknown formula that guarantees advertising with a high ROI is still controversial today.

In 2016, insurer Metlife asked us to take a deeper look into its advertising test data to better understand what makes advertising successful. In 2017, we then developed the method further for this purpose and tested it extensively in six sectors.

Subsequently, I was invited to speak at several conferences. While my presentations to market researchers were received with (restrained) interest, the feedback from the "creative" audience was rather poor.

I still remember the final presentation at the Shoppers Brain Conference in Amsterdam. The presentations were evaluated afterwards by the participants using an app and as I was the last one, I was hoping for particularly good feedback. After all, in my presentation I showed a clear method of how advertising can be optimized holistically and systematically for the first time.

The result was a "kick in the butt" for my ego. It was the worst feedback I've ever received. The slightly agitated questions from the audience after the presentation should have given me pause for thought.

If I had told on stage that there will soon be an AI that could write great texts and produce photos and videos without being distinguishable from the real thing, the audience would have laughed out loud.

It is the self-image of creative people that they cannot be replaced by mechanics. Interestingly, I even agree with this in essence. But you have to understand what is really "creative" in the creative process and what is just the application of beliefs, smoke and mirrors and outdated pseudo-knowledge.

The creative spark and holistic inspiration will define us as humans for a long time to come. I believe that people who know how to use AI can be more creative and more effective - not less.

But back to the process, which uses Causal AI to distil what makes advertising successful and which specific guidelines can be used to significantly increase ROI. The methodology, which we have named Creative.AI, consists of three components:

1. advertising test: In a survey, we measure the emotional reaction to the advertisement, the willingness to buy the product, the brand strength and some other typical indicators of an advertising test.

2. profiling: Using a coding rule that we have adopted from the company 602 Communications, one of our employees looks at the advertising and categorizes its content according to around 200 characteristics. These characteristics are the story structure (e.g. problem-solution sequence), the stereotypical message (e.g. this brand is your friend) and the advertising techniques (e.g. voiceover, expert or brand song).

3. causal AI: The characteristics of an advertisement evoke an emotional response, which in turn triggers brand acceptance and ultimately purchase intent.

It turns out that causal AI can **explain** the willingness to buy about **three times better** than statistical modeling. Both the way in which we test advertising and the way in which we profile it could still be improved today. What is crucial about the approach, however, is that it does not stop at perception as before, but takes up the actual characteristics of advertising.

Most exciting are the findings that the methodology has brought to light in many industry studies. Generally valid, recurring and industry-specific findings emerged:

It is universal that advertising works by giving pleasure in some way. Advertising that triggers negative emotions such as anger, disgust or contempt is usually a waste of money. Such emotions can easily be triggered unintentionally. For example, when a meat eater sees someone biting into a vegetarian sausage (which back then was not as meat-like as it is today), many of the meat eaters watching feel "disgust". This reaction prevents any positive advertising effect.

Many advertising techniques are also universal in their effect. Here are a few examples: The voiceover technique confuses the viewer. If the consumer is supposed to learn something specific in the commercial, it is best to show a speaker who speaks the message in clear words into the camera. The most effective technique to make the viewer happy is the "looser trick". This is the same trick that Laurel & Hardy or Tom & Jerry have been using for 100 years. There is one person in the commercial who is laughed at because something happens to them or they are clumsy.

However, the emotional messages of the commercial are industry-specific. For example, spirits are usually advertised in a way that emphasizes their quality or the fun in the company of others. However, the promise of indulgence is the most effective theme spirit brands needs to play. For investment products, the message "We are like a friend at your side" is the most effective.

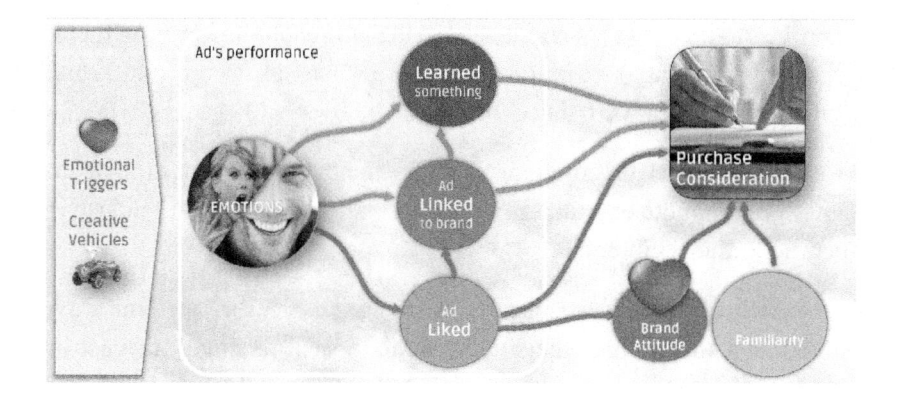

From this very brief description it is already clear that this is by no means a blueprint for an advertisement. They are guidelines that a creative person can fill in with their work. It is more of a lighthouse that ensures that you navigate safely in the right direction.

Our research approach based on causal AI has never gained wider acceptance. When I met Jon Puleston again last year, who is Director of Innovation at Kantar, I realized why that is. Kantar itself runs an advertising testing methodology called LINK and has a large department of data scientists. They have now developed a methodology they call LINK.AI. They use deep learning AI systems to automatically categorize advertising into several hundred properties. An AI model is then trained based on a huge database of past advertising tests. With this AI model, Kantar can now predict the results of advertising test surveys quite well, making the advertising test redundant.

The product sells "like hot cakes". It sells so well that Kantar has made advertising tests mandatory for all those who want to use the prediction in order to obtain more learning data.

When I heard about this, I realized where the need really lies. Decision-makers want a forecast. They want to know whether an ad is good or not. Kantar delivers that. What it doesn't do is describe what would increase success instead. This is not (yet) a good sell. Because these statements are then in conflict with what the "creatives" say. But who knows how things will develop? We will come back to this in context of Gen AI.

Marketing Strategy

After several successful Causal AI projects at Deutsche Telekom, I received an email from T-Mobile USA in the summer of 2013. David, the Insights Director at the time, told me that the new brand and product strategy was working wonders and spurring growth. What was giving them a headache, however, was that T-Mobile didn't know what exactly was attracting customers. Was it the then innovative flat rate? Was it the fact that T-Mobile had completely removed the contract commitment? Or was it the fact that it came with an iPhone for USD 0?

We had the opportunity to take a closer look at the extensive brand tracking data to better understand what drives customer behavior. On the day I presented our findings, I was a little unsure whether David would be satisfied with the depth of the insights. I didn't realize that the results would have such a big impact on the future of the company and the group as a whole. Just before Christmas, I received this thank you email from David:

> agencies to think outside of the box. It was fortuitous that you connected with me because I identified immediately with your approach and it aligned well with the evolution in my own thinking.
>
> You can't believe how impactful the work that you are doing has been. It is informing high-level strategy, tactical messaging decisions, and serving as an arbiter of 'truth.' And with each additional slice or dice we do, it continues to add value and enhance our confidence in the face validity of the information. I've attached a few draft decks for you to see how we are beginning to communicate the results.
>
> And so I want to thank you for pushing us daily and for being patient with us as we learn how to apply the approach.
>
> I wish you and your family a fantastic Christmas and a very Happy New Year.
>
> Best wishes!
>
> David Feick
> Director, Consumer Insights, MSO
>
> T··Mobile·
> 12920 SE 38ᵗʰ St | Bellevue, WA 98006
> Direct 425.383.7275 | Mobile 415.596.4926 | david.feick@t-mobile.com

What had happened? Our analysis had shown that none of the presumed success drivers were directly responsible for the growth. Instead, it turned out that the company's positioning as the "Robin Hood" of the industry was the key lever for success. The innovations "no contract commitment", "flat rate", "good and affordable devices" were the perfect arguments to make this positioning credible. They had an indirect effect and reinforced the positioning. Each of these elements could be copied. The Robin Hood status was not. So the brand decided to develop a continuous stream of unusual features and launch new ones every quarter. One example was the "Free Global Roaming" feature. The approach became known as "Uncarrier Moves".

The strategy worked. T-Mobile grew year on year and took over its competitor Sprint seven years later. Today, the brand has risen from a small, loss-making provider with inferior mobile networks to become the market-leading, highly profitable mobile communications company in the USA.

In 2022, I met Tim Höttges, CEO of Deutsche Telekom, at his keynote speech (picture below). What he showed there put the icing on the cake. The parent company has risen from being the seventh-largest telecommunications group in the world to number one largely thanks to the development of T-Mobile USA.

It's amazing what the results of a Causal AI analysis can do. Today I think: We should have invested our fee in T-Mobile shares. But well, what could be better than having your recommendations implemented?

This is a prime example of how marketing strategies should be well-founded. I had already shown similar examples in the previous chapter, e.g. from Kindernothilfe. These examples show that it is worthwhile for every sector to take another look at its own understanding of the market.

For the German beer market, for example, we have found that it is not the quality or the special taste, but the promise of refreshment that makes the basic benefit of a pilsner. We also found out that the purchase of body care products (shower gel etc.) is most sustainably influenced by the fragrance experience. Both are plausible findings, but they are not mainstream.

There are probably thousands of methods and variations to understand what motivates the buyer of a product category. Many of them complement each other, some are more useful than others. What most of them have in common is that they deliver plausible results. Therein lies the danger. Because people tend to use plausibility as an indicator of truth. However, plausibility only expresses whether something is congruent with existing prior knowledge. That doesn't really help if you want to learn something.

There are many methods that claim to uncover the "why" behind customer behavior. Very few of them have the scientific ideal of causality in mind. That is why there is no perceived lack of "why" explanations. Our brain generates them automatically anyway. It's like with sports. The fans always know why things aren't going well. That's just how our brain works.

However, I hope that these examples give some indication that it is worth approaching the question of "why" in a exploratory but quantitative way. The benefits of Causal AI for marketing strategy can be summarized as follows:

- **Holistic**: Existing expert knowledge is used to set up the model optimally instead of just challenging the results as before.
- **Fills the gap**: There is a methodological gap between qualitative research and quantitative modeling (which takes a confirmatory approach). Causal AI fills this gap by proceeding

with explorative but knowledge-based and quantitative but unrestricted discovery.
- **Networked**: Causal AI inherently models the networking of all system variables instead of assuming a reductionist input-output relationship. As a result, causal effects are measured holistically instead of identifying only partial effects, as is usually the case.
- **Complexity-affirming**: Causal AI can (if used correctly) uncover unknown non-linearities and unknown interactions of all kinds and thus enable a deeper qualitative understanding.
- **Validatable**: In contrast to qualitative research approaches, validity is measurable, reproducible and therefore comparable.

The greatest leverage lies in explaining the reasons behind success and failure. Causal AI delivers this "why" in a quality that no other methodology can. Unfortunately, many decision-makers do not realize that plausibility is a weak predictor of truth. This is why there is no urgent demand for answers to the "why" in many companies. Because "answers" are a dime a dozen. Whether they are valid is another matter. Decision-makers who can separate the wheat from the chaff here have a strategic advantage, as the examples have hopefully illustrated.

DECIDE better with Causal AI

The situation is different when it comes to operational decisions. Here, the success of the decision can often be measured in real time. When AI came back into fashion after another "AI winter" in the 2010s, it was almost always about predictive analytics. The aim is to use AI to make better and more flexible operational decisions.

What are operational decisions? In marketing, we can distinguish between two types of decisions: Firstly, decisions that affect communication, product, packaging and distribution. These decisions affect **ALL** customers. On the other hand, there are customer-specific decisions that can be found in direct marketing, sales, customer service and customer management, where **a separate decision** can be made **for each customer.**

Better Decisions on Communication, Products & Packaging

Which advertising idea should be implemented? Which new product concept should be introduced? Which packaging design is best received? Which price maximizes profit?

Decisions of this kind are primarily evaluated using test surveys. AI can be used to predict the outcome of the survey. By applying causal AI, such a model can be made more stable so that the predictions are actually more valid and more likely to occur. Some examples have already been mentioned.

For example, Kantar's "Link" model, which predicts the results of an advertising test. With the help of Causal AI, such a model could achieve better forecasting performance on live data in the future. This is because Causal AI models suffer less from model drift, as they not only interpret the characteristics of the advertising causally better, but also include or control confounders.

One example is the New Product Forecasting Model that we built for Mintel. It enables an initial screening of new products before the actual market launch. With a success rate of 81 percent, the model is very useful.

Deep learning systems (providers such as Aimpower or Neurons) that use image information to predict the results of real eye tracking studies have already been established for testing ads and videos in particular. It is already possible to predict with an accuracy of 90% where consumers will look at images and for how long. Of course, there are borderline areas where this does not yet work so well.

For example, the AI knows that people like to look at faces, but it has not learned that dog owners like to look dogs in the eye just as much. Another example is the "black square" painting. People are looking at the edges, while the AI assumes that the gaze is in the center. These examples show that this AI lacks the contextual information that a causal AI would ideally take into account. Further developments through causal AI can be expected here in the future.

Better Decisions on Personalized Actions

The procedure is described easily. Lets take churn prediction again. In the first step, the customer data is prepared in such a way that the customer's current characteristics and behavioral data from one year ago are used as predictor variables. The target variable examined is whether the customer canceled the contract in the following period. The model should learn to predict these churns. The AI can access thousands of customer data records to create a prediction model.

The trained AI model is then used to carry out the churn scoring of all customers itself. Only the same feature variables are updated for this purpose. The model was trained with characteristics dating back one year. The AI model uses this to calculate a pseudo churn probability -

a value between 0 and 1. For various reasons, this value is not a "real" probability.

As the value does not represent a "real" probability, it is still necessary to define the threshold value above which an action is to be triggered that attempts to prevent churn.

As mentioned in the first chapter, every churn prediction model makes two types of errors: false alarms or missed opportunities. In the case of a false alarm, churn is predicted even though it will not occur. The costs for the campaign were therefore spent in vain. In the case of a missed opportunity, the model fails to predict churn. The customer is lost.

If we set the threshold value to just 0.1, we will consider most customers to be churners. This will minimize the error of the missed opportunity, but the error of false alarms will be very large.

If we set the threshold value to 0.9, we only have a few false alarms. But the missed opportunities are increasing.

The optimum threshold value can only be determined if I know how much an action costs, how likely it is to prevent a cancellation and how much customer value is lost if a customer cancels. By simulating the ROI for all possible threshold values, the ROI can be optimized.

Campaign management

Back to the example of the telecommunications company. The question arose as to how effective the cuddle calls actually were.

The properties of the model can be revealed using the simulation techniques described in the previous chapter. In this example, we were able to show that the cuddle calls were actually useful. The calls were increasingly answered by people who were at home during the day. It turned out that these people had a higher cancellation rate per se. However, of those who would have accepted a call, fewer canceled among those who had accepted the call.

How is the evaluation of measures (campaign management) usually carried out today? Exactly the same as with our telecommunications company. The number of callers is compared between those called and those not called. The example shows that this type of control works only accidently - at best.

Proper campaign management requires causal AI. This not only allows us to measure how much a campaign reduces the likelihood of churn. We can carry out this simulation for each individual customer. The effect can be greater for some customers than for others. Especially if the number of customers above the threshold is greater than the budget would allow. In this case, the customers for whom the planned measure is particularly effective are selected.

This shows that a forecast should ideally not be viewed in isolation from the planned actions. After all, the aim of the churn forecast is to carry out actions that avoid churn.

Customer Lifetime Value

Customer lifetime value has been a hot topic in marketing literature for thirty years, but hardly any company goes beyond a current sales or margin analysis. The reason for this is a lack of information about how likely it is that the customer will remain a customer in the future and how high the annual recommendation rate is.

A practicable customer lifetime value can be calculated if a number of churn forecast models are used in parallel. One that predicts cancellations in one year. Another for the second year. Another for the third year. And so on.

Alternatively, a forecasting model can also predict the sales or margin contribution that the customer will make in each of the future years.

The future years must then be discounted using the opportunity interest rate. The sum of all these values gives the customer value.

This customer value is in turn useful in many applications. In particular, it is needed when searching for the optimal threshold value of the churn model in order to correctly take into account the opportunity costs of the "missed opportunity".

The advantages of causal AI for supporting operational decisions can be summarized as follows:

- **Stable over time:** Lapse models in particular are trained with data that is one year old. Causal AI are more time-stable models that suffer less from model drift. Therefore, current predictions are working better.
- **Suitable for campaign management:** The question of the influence of an action on the target value is a causal question that Causal AI can answer better. This means that the predictions about the consequences of an action are also more valid.

GENERATE better with Causal AI

Generative AI is so much in the spotlight today that people often talk about "artificial intelligence" when they actually mean generative AI. The fields of application are diverse. The potential is only just being explored.

However, this sounding out reveals a peculiarity of us humans. We generate marketing texts, we generate advertising images and evaluate the results with our subjective impression. Is the result plausible? Does it make a "good impression"? This type of assessment is justified, but it also has many blind spots.

Anyone who has played with ChatGPT has had to realize that the results change greatly depending on how you "prompt" the system. Can we use causal AI to figure out how to prompt to generate marketing material that works better?

Generate Better Ads

Dr. Steffen Schmidt is a marketing researcher like no other. He is constantly testing and combining the latest tools. When he sat among the participants at our first Causal AI seminar in 2009, it was immediately clear to me. Since then, he has been one of the pioneers in the application of our technology in market research. In 2023, he skillfully combined Causal AI with various Gen AI tools and massively improved the impact of Social Media Ads for Samsung. Here's how he went about it:

Step 1 - Causal AI: He conducted a survey among smartphone users and measured which brand archetypes customers associate with the respective brands. He fed the data into a causal AI model to find out which brand archetypes increase the willingness to buy a smartphone. The strongest factor was "Explorer", although (or precisely because) most brands are not perceived as Explorers.

Step 2 - Gen AI: He then asked ChatGPT to write a prompt for Midjourney to produce a social media ad for a particular SAMSUNG phone expressing the Explorer archetype. Without further choice, he accepted Midjourney's suggestion. He generated the tagline using the Neuroflash app - an application specifically designed for generating advertising copy. The result was the slogan "The freedom to go further".

Step 3 - Test: With the InContext market research solution, respondents experience Instagram, Facebook, TikTok or Amazon as if they were visiting them in real life. The solution uses a clone of the website and can therefore replace the advertising at will. After one minute, a survey that takes the response time into account measures the willingness to buy the Samsung brand. The comparison with conventional advertising showed an 18 percent higher market share for Samsung.

The result is amazing. The creation process did not require any advertising expertise. A very standardizable process combining Causal AI and Gen AI was used. Without further optimization, an increase in performance was achieved that would have required a lot of work, variants and test loops under conventional circumstances and would never have been implemented due to budget constraints.

The example is so powerful because the market researchers are not sufficiently successful in briefing the creatives so that creatives implement the results in the way market researcher did not intend.

I have experienced this myself time and again. Creative agencies often have a completely different understanding of what is written in the market researchers' recommendations. What is an explorer archetype? How do you visualize it? Qualitative summaries often offer so much room for interpretation that the effect is lost.

Gen AI offers a standardizable and validatable interpretation mechanism. This is exactly what the manual process of a creative agency cannot provide.

While Causal AI is the more valid method for generating insights, Gen AI is the more valid method for creatively translating them into marketing material.

Will humans become redundant? Not at all! Humans are taking the helm. With their knowledge and wisdom, they orchestrate both Causal AI and the control of Gen AI.

Marketing professionals quickly realized that although Gen AI can produce beautiful ads, the brand is not recognized in them in case of doubt because the design brand assets are not used. There are solutions to this and other weaknesses. For example, the addition in Midjourney *--sref "URL"* can provide the AI with an image and color language that the AI can use to create recognition.

Where Causal AI consists of AI, filter algorithms and specialist knowledge, a functioning creative system consists of GenAI, Causal AI and specialist knowledge.

<u>Creative AI = Gene AI + Causal AI + Expert knowledge</u>

Generate Better Copy

The effectiveness of emails, letters and websites is largely determined by effective texts. This involves the right topics and arguments on the one hand and the right tonality and metaphors on the other.

To make Success Drivers' own emails more effective, we experimented with the combination of Causal AI and LLMs in 2020. The latter already existed in the form of GPT2, among others. Our process should increase the open rates of our emails by no less than 500%.

Step 1 - Expert Judgement - We designed 50 variants for subject lines and had them evaluated by experts. The best and worst variants were tested in real mailings. As a result, the variants rated as poor were better than the supposedly good ones.

Step 2 - Trial & error: Now we got creative and tested the craziest variants in small random samples in real mailings. The resulting opening rates were to serve as the target variable for the next optimization step.

Step 3 - Optimization: At first, the subject lines were broken down into basic associations and categorized using natural language processing using the Neuroflash App. This categorization then served as input for the causal AI. This showed that a dominant language encourages recipients to open. We then prompted the LLMs (with the help of the then already existing Neuroflash tool) to suggest subject lines that were dominant but no longer than five words. The "straight to the point" subject line proved to be a direct hit. Open rates of 54%, previously thought impossible, became reality.

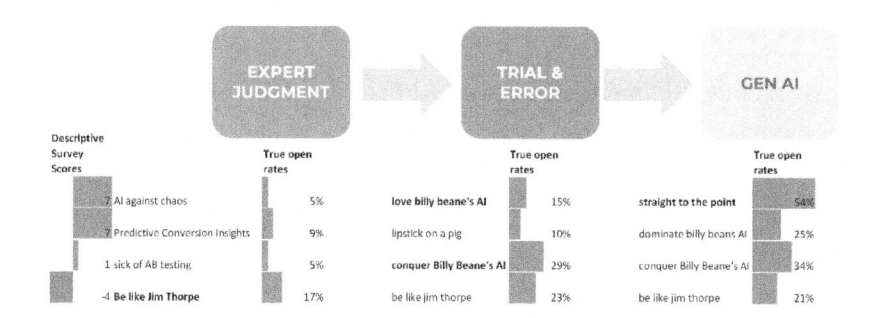

	EXPERT JUDGMENT		TRIAL & ERROR		GEN AI	
Descriptive Survey Scores		True open rates		True open rates		True open rates
7 AI against chaos		5%	love billy beane's AI	15%	straight to the point	54%
7 Predictive Conversion Insights		9%	lipstick on a pig	10%	dominate billy beans AI	25%
1 sick of AB testing		5%	conquer Billy Beane's AI	29%	conquer Billy Beane's AI	34%
-4 Be like Jim Thorpe		17%	be like jim thorpe	23%	be like jim thorpe	21%

The same process is used to optimize newsletter headlines, texts, mailings or website headlines. The largest possible number of examples is required from which the AI can learn. The number of variants is more important than the sample size per variant. For example, we only sent 50 emails per subject line and were thus able to test 40 variants simultaneously with 2000 recipients.

ChatGPT is known for writing great texts and responding to the user's wishes. But how do we know whether their requests lead to effective variants? This is precisely the evidence provided by a Causal AI-driven process.

Sounds complicated? Yes, it is not simple. But can you calculate the impact if a campaign improves by just 10%? What is the absolute additional profit? Probably more than ten times the investment in weeks. It quickly becomes clear that these AI-based processes pay for themselves very quickly.

The benefits of Causal AI

Causal AI helps to become more efficient in all areas of marketing. It is a kind of AI upgrade that makes insights, decisions and creation more efficient.

Better insights

In marketing mix modeling, causal AI helps to get an analytical handle on the increasingly correlated channels. Their influence is determined more realistically and at the same time indirect effects, which are reflected in long-term effects among other things, are taken into account.

The drivers of the customer experience can be better understood. The application of Causal AI overcomes the fallacy that the topics most frequently mentioned by customers are also the most relevant. It makes it possible to simulate the financial impact of improving the customer experience.

Causal AI gives product innovation and optimization new methodological possibilities to find out which product characteristics and barriers play a central role in purchase intention and willingness to pay. This means that you are no longer limited by the small number of features of Conjoint or the explicit survey methodology of MaxDiff.

The impact of communication and advertising can be better understood through Causal AI. This deeper understanding goes far beyond the aspects that are queried in an advertising test. It is revealing to understand which emotions are "deadly" or what contribution brand building makes. It is particularly useful if the analysis can provide recommendations for the storyline, the emotional message, the choice of music or the type of humor.

A marketing strategy requires effective positioning, target group selection and segmentation. Causal AI can provide insights based on appropriate surveys to deliver effective brand positioning both in terms of content and association/emotion and to understand which customer types have an affinity for the product category.

Better decisions.

Causal AI is also used to create forecasts. However, these models are more stable and less susceptible to model drift. They also reduce the risk of discrimination against minorities.

When it comes to selecting products, advertising or packaging design, a Causal AI model can in some cases replace testing through market research or trial and error. This allows decisions to be made more quickly and cost-effectively.

When it comes to direct marketing or customer service campaigns, an individual decision can be made for each customer and target customer as to which marketing campaign should be used. This decision can be optimized using causal AI. Examples of this include reducing cancellation rates, estimating customer potential or customer lifetime value.

Better creation

Generative AI supports marketing in the creation of images, videos and texts. The contribution that Causal AI can make is to ensure that from the almost infinite possibilities, a variant is found that is highly likely to be highly effective, not just plausible.

More effective advertising motifs can be generated by feeding Causal AI on the basis of suitable market research, which then identifies which content and emotional-associative characteristics the image must express in order to be effective.

Effective messages are needed, for example, on websites, in subject lines or mailing headlines and in slogans. This can be optimized with causal AI by trying out many different variants in real experiments. By breaking down texts into their associative factors, Causal AI can identify the hidden characteristics of effective texts. With this knowledge, Gen AI can then be used to generate new, more effective texts.

Benefits = Better insights + Better decisions + Better creation

Chapter 5

THE DOING

How you can win over your organization for this task

When I talk to managers of large companies, I always realize one thing. The big problem is often not finding out what could be done better. Rather, it's about getting the organization on board and convincing them to try out a better solution, implement it and use the results systematically.

Many of our customers are much more experienced in this area than I am. I am just summarizing here what I have learned from the pioneers in marketing for large companies.

I have noticed three areas that need to be considered if you want to implement the right methodology as an internal pioneer:

1. What conditions must be created for the solution to be accepted?

2. Who do you have to convince to take the entire organization with you?

3. How can you proceed to convince?

How to Proceed

Introducing a new solution in a company is like launching an innovative product on the market. Adoption research has dealt intensively with this problem and identified eight universal reasons for the failure of innovations.

After publishing an early version of our Causal AI method in a peer-reviewed journal in 2008, I started helping companies as well as PhD and Master's students to use the software. One of the master's students was Daniel. He was doing his master's degree part-time while working at a telecommunications company on the implementation of mobile payment solutions. I learned all about the eight adoption barriers from Daniel as he built a Causal AI model.

In fact, the model showed something unexpected for me. It wasn't the benefits or the simplicity of the product that was the problem with customer acceptance. Mobile payments just weren't "the process" and didn't fit with the way people were used to paying for purchases. This change in familiar processes was the biggest obstacle to the product's growth.

Since then, we at Success Drivers have been using these eight criteria to evaluate new products. The introduction of Causal AI in your company is also a question of adoption and it makes sense to optimize this task along the following eight aspects:

1. Benefit: Does Causal AI solve a real problem?

2. Certainty: Is the buyer sure that the effort and investment in Causal AI is worthwhile?

3. Uniqueness: Does the impression arise that "this already exists" or "we've done this before"?

4. Usability: Is the solution easy to use?

5. Quick start: Can a quick benefit be achieved with a small investment of time?

6. Does it fit into existing processes? Or does the company have to learn to work in completely new processes?

7. Appealing design: Do you like the aesthetics or does the design make you uncomfortable?

8. Trusted brand: Is the solution offered by a trusted brand?

The importance of the eight factors varies depending on the product category. For causal AI, all eight factors are certainly of some relevance. In my experience, however, the first three factors are the most important:

Adoption drivers: Benefits

I often give talks on the topic of causal AI in marketing. Among other things, I often speak at fundraising conferences. In discussions with fundraisers, one argument has proven to be particularly effective. The decision-makers were already aware that we could help them make better decisions or improve customer loyalty.

But what really struck home was this argument: NGOs manage donations and have to use them to pay for their marketing and sales (fundraising). Every Euro that is invested inefficiently does not benefit charitable causes. It is therefore negligent not to use causal AI in fundraising, and looking at ROI rather than pure costs is a moral duty for fundraisers. With this argument, I have gotten to the heart of the existing problem. It is also important to understand what is subjectively perceived as a benefit.

In this book, I have tried to show the advantages of the Causal AI methodology. Which of them solve a problem that actually exists for you? That can change depending on the situation.

Have you just noticed that certain forecasting systems are losing performance? Then highlight the benefits of avoiding model drift.

Is discrimination by AI a hot topic? Then focus on it.

Or is it a problem that the insights of existing systems have led to actions and initiatives that show little success? Then Causal AI could offer the solution here.

Do your areas of application lie in the discovery of strategic insights, in the creation of automated individual marketing decisions such as retention measures? Or is there a need for more effective generation of marketing material through AI, enabled by causal AI?

It is crucial to find a problem area and a field of application that addresses a real problem. A real problem is a topic where a credible solution option always falls on open ears. "Oh, that's possible?" is the question you hear when you propose such a solution.

Adoption driver: certainty

Isn't the problem with today's marketing that customers no longer believe anything? After all, we are bombarded with unbelievable claims every day. Many customers have learned for themselves that you can't really believe the promises of marketing. Everything is perceived to be "inflated", decisive factors are exaggerated or omitted.

As a result, marketing as a source of information is becoming increasingly difficult. Content marketing has evolved from this. Peer-to-peer networks are sprouting up. People believe their colleagues more.

If you doubt the benefit, the actual perceived benefit is low. You can boil it down to a formula:

Want to have = Benefit minus Effort times Certainty

This is precisely why a pilot project is usually a good idea. However, it must be designed in such a way that the benefits can actually be experienced. It should be set up with the intention of building the full version if it is successful. This presupposes that the relevant people are involved in the pilot so that the requirements of the organization are already clear in the pilot.

Adoption driver: Uniqueness

Before the streaming speaker brand SONOS launched its Move and Roam mobile models, we at Success Drivers had the pleasure of testing the product "in the market" with a survey. We determined the implicit willingness to pay (Implicit Price Intelligence) and how the product was perceived on the eight Adoption Drivers. Causal AI then showed that willingness to buy and willingness to pay increased significantly when consumers perceived the product as unique. It turned out that most target customers did not understand the specific difference to conventional Bluetooth speakers. This was the biggest obstacle to the product launch.

By placing the Wifi functionality at the center of the communication, Sonos made the launch a complete success.

I think it's similar with the introduction of causal AI. Many data scientists simply don't know anything about it. There are many statistical methods that purport to measure the effect of a cause. I still get asked sometimes if correlation wouldn't be enough.

Multivariate regression is still very often used and sold today as "driver analysis". If it is important for companies to also capture non-linearities, many market research agencies resort to Shapley value regression, although scientific studies show that this method delivers misleading results.

Recently, market research software providers have been offering an "AI Driver Analysis". This consists of a random forest method and an impact measurement borrowed from Explainable AI. Anyone who has not dealt with the requirements for causality may well be confused by the plethora of methods. This is because they all claim to measure the influence of causes. That is the reason why I am writing this book. I want to make clear what it takes to understand what drives success (causality).

A random forest approach (or another common AI approach) does not meet the requirements that we developed in the third chapter. The more strongly the drivers correlate with each other, the more distorted and therefore unusable the results become.

Who to Target

When David from T-Mobile USA commissioned us back then, it was primarily his initiative and decision. Of course, he asked his boss for permission, but she trusted him and didn't start her own evaluation. He listened to everything in two online meetings with me and discussed his challenges with me. After that, it was clear to him that he wanted to pilot the method. The results were so convincing that he had a retainer fitted.

After all these years, I've always wondered what kind of people want to try out Causal AI without months of internal discussions. I think the term "early adopter" sums it up best. For most people - including managers - it's not enough to find something plausible or have proof of its effectiveness. They need social support (in B2B: the organization). References alone are not enough either. "They all have logo wallpapers," is the response.

According to marketing literature, around 15% of people are early adopter types. These are people for whom their own professional judgment is enough to decide whether something makes sense and should be tried out.

When I presented our work with SONOS at the 2018 ESOMAR Congress, the head of market research at Microsoft - Reed Cundiff - was on the panel that selected the presentations. He immediately realized that our technology could help Microsoft.

"If the head of one of the largest market research departments in the world gives his department heads a tip, it will be done", you might think. But in my experience, that's not how it works. For good reason, line managers hardly interfere in the work of their teams, who then find ways to "get rid of" projects that, in their view, bring little added value.

Once again, we were lucky that another early adopter - Dr. Rajul Jain - had taken over the testing of our method. She was so convinced of the methodology that she did the internal persuasion work with great commitment.

In my view, it is therefore crucial to identify early adopters in the company. You need these people to gain a foothold in a larger company.

If you are an early adopter yourself, you would do well to find allied early adopters. This can slowly create a critical mass that encourages the sluggish masses to follow.

If your company is so big that you can't get a good idea of all your colleagues, ChatGPT can actually help (no joke!) We tried it ourselves once. We used the LinkedIn Navigator to find 1000 people who belong to the target group. Then we searched for each person's self-description in LinkedIn and asked ChatGPT to what extent this person is an early adapter of our service. The 50 people with the highest scores received a book from me in the mail with a cover letter.

I know from experience that such mailings are very rarely followed by replies or even project inquiries. This time it was different. We immediately received a project briefing from a large company. Our offer was convincing and we carried out our first joint project.

How to Convince

Persuasion is a tricky business, because it involves "imposing" an opinion on someone - even if you mean well. To exaggerate, it is essentially about the attitude of the knowledgeable person who wants to convert the ignorant. But nobody wants to be converted against their will. People sense this, no matter how sophisticated the tactics.

That's why, in my view, your own attitude is crucial. I like to ask myself the question: "Can I bear to let the other person have their opinion, even if I don't like it? Respect for others means giving them the freedom to choose. And even more. It is regularly helpful to remind ourselves to be humble. Because the more convinced we are ourselves, the more blind we can become to completely different points of view. Views that may later prove to be wiser than our own.

With humility and respect, we can go into the process with the intention of inspiring. This will be more fruitful in the long term than narrow-minded persuasion.

Interests

When I drive through my adopted home of Cologne, I see a Ford B-Max on the road every day. How can that be? Production of this model was discontinued in 2017 due to a lack of demand. My wife has been driving the car for 10 years and I find it super practical. The lack of a B-pillar and the sliding doors are just great. As I am a self-confessed (lonely) fan of this car, I notice this model every day.

This is known as the "cocktail party effect". Our subconscious filters the available information and makes us aware of those that it considers relevant.

This process is constantly active, even when we are listening to someone giving a lecture. Studies show that only around 5% of what is said is remembered. These are mainly the arguments and information that our subconscious plays back to us.

What information is this? It is information that appears to be "relevant" to us in some way. In other words: **Perception is interest-driven**. If I am a CFO who wants to have a profit at the end of the year, then I am interested in everything measurable that contributes to this profit.

If I am a creative brand manager who "knows" that creative performance is difficult to measure, then I am interested in arguments that support my point of view.

So if I want to inspire someone to think outside the box, I should show how my thesis serves their interests. The reference to their interests makes the argument relevant and is then examined.

An early adopter is interested in an objectively better solution. A CFO is interested in a solution that delivers demonstrable and risk-free bottom-line results. A team leader who is to be promoted to another team in two years is interested in results that show visible success after one year.

It is actually trivial, but it is work to put yourself in people's shoes and find out where their interests lie. It may be trivial, but it contradicts our world view that we should all be professional and objective and therefore all serve the same corporate goal. Putting this into perspective is an important step in being able to inspire colleagues.

Case studies

I have spent 20 years - including my doctorate - in the education system. The didactic method of science is deductive. This means that a theory or thesis is first discussed abstractly and then concrete examples are derived from it. The way people learn is exactly the opposite. Learning is inductive. It starts with examples. Only when we have heard at least one are we ready to absorb the general learning from it.

As far as it made sense to me (and I was attentive enough), I have done exactly that in this book. First the example, then the lesson. I am also deeply convinced from my own professional life that the presentation of theses is not understood without prior examples. Because "understanding" means relating abstract knowledge to other concrete knowledge. This is how it becomes conceivable.

I myself am a victim of my educational path and try to get a little better every day. Do the same! Your audience will thank you for it.

Storytelling

The story is the refinement of a case study. Mankind has always been preoccupied with the question of how events can be presented in such a way that the audience listens attentively to a story. The basic structure of an optimal story has not changed since the ancient Greeks.

The art of storytelling was cultivated by the ancient Greeks and continues to be practiced professionally in the film industry. In recent years, management writers have taken up this art and transferred it to the world of management.

There are great books on this, which I cannot summarize perfectly here. Essentially, however, the point is that case studies need some central stylistic devices and a dramaturgy.

As a stylistic device, we need a hero who is as "likable" as possible, a person with whom the audience can identify. You also need a villain who has to be defeated.

The dramaturgy classically begins in a state of equilibrium, which is immediately followed by a catastrophic event. This is the entrepreneurial challenge. The resulting suffering is then attempted to be overcome with the help of a solution. But the first attempt fails. The tension mounts. This "attempt to solve" and failure can be repeated several times in a dramaturgy. Finally, there is a finale in which the hero confronts the villain (who defends the challenge) with a new solution and finally wins (eliminates the challenge).

Anyone who succeeds in packing case studies into such stories captivates the audience, entertains them and wins their hearts.

Evidence and safety

At the beginning of my career, I was Marketing & Sales Director at the global market leader for industrial packaging. In this role, I was also responsible for innovation. We developed new industrial drums and transport solutions. I even have registered a patent for a transport solution. It was not easy to find early adopters on the customer side. That's why I concentrated on clearly communicating and demonstrating the added value of the solutions.

In this process, it was only over the years that I realized that something else was much more important in the industry than offering better products and services. Customers often put dangerous or expensive products in the packaging. Every leak and every accident was a nightmare for everyone involved. Moreover, packaging was only a minor cost factor. If the production process was disrupted by packaging or logistics, the costs were many times higher. Safety and reliability were the be-all and end-all. That was the "language" of the industry. Continuity, brand, reliability and quality were the attributes of the winners.

The limbic center of the brain plays an important role in what we call the subconscious. It turns out that people react with different affinities to certain limbic motivators. Brain research has identified three dimensions that drive all people: stimulation, dominance and balance.

Early adopters are particularly attracted to the new, to innovation. This releases dopamine. The topic is exciting and thrilling. Stimulation is the preferred motivator. This is why early adopters are the first target group for innovations such as Causal AI.

Leaders are attracted to the best and to performance. They release testosterone and seek success and prestige. Dominance is the preferred motivator. People with strong leadership skills are usually managers.

Protectors and caregivers are attracted to security, harmony and balance. Oxytocin is released and a feeling of home, security and love is conveyed. Balance is the preferred motivator.

Everyone has their inclinations and these also lead to a career choice. In order to successfully promote innovation in a company, all three aspects must be addressed. The aspect of the new is inevitably linked to innovation.

To inspire the traditional manager, more needs to be added: evidence, i.e. proof of performance. What are the factual advantages of the solution? How can they be translated into performance indicators that are important for the decision-maker? These are the questions that need to be answered in order to inspire performance and results-oriented decision-makers.

We need results from comparative studies that clearly demonstrate the superiority of causal AI. Depending on the use case - discovering vs. deciding vs. generating - the comparative studies must be structured differently.

The advantages of causal AI "model drift" and "discrimination" both address the issue of risk avoidance and safety maintenance. Depending on the contact person, they are therefore only motivating for a specific target group.

Metaphor

If you have read this book carefully, you will have noticed many metaphors. Wherever possible, I have tried to organize the chapters according to the pattern "Story > Learning > Metaphor".

I was inspired by Oliver Raskin. He is currently Head of Insights at MIRO. Oliver told me about his "superpower" at a dinner together when we were talking about how Insights can gain a foothold in the company.

"Whenever possible, I summarize everything in a metaphor," he said and told me how this often works wonders.

We are often dealing with very abstract things. "Causal AI" - what could be more abstract? It makes sense to use a simile to give the whole thing an image. Because what does understanding mean? Understanding is the process of relating something new to known units of knowledge. The more concretely these units of knowledge are anchored, the more comprehensible the statement becomes. Images are very concrete units of knowledge.

It's like trying to build a house out of bricks. If the stones are soft, made of cotton candy or soft lumps of slime, the house won't hold. Solid stones made of concrete are like concrete pictures. They create a solid house, an understandable statement.

A picture is worth a thousand words.

Role model

In 2022, we had started to market our pricing method "Implicit Price Intelligence" as a DIY tool. Then I had an idea. We invited our target group to a webinar where each participant had to take part in a 5-minute survey as a prerequisite for access. Our tool itself was used in this survey and the target group's willingness to pay for the tool was measured. I then presented the procedure and the results in the webinar - along with the agreed price change. The price was increased by 20 percent for frequent buyers, but reduced by 30 percent for newcomers.

"Drink your own wine", as the saying goes.

It makes intuitive sense. But is that really necessary?

Convincing others is a difficult game. You can deceive and manipulate. Or you can adapt to your counterpart for nobler motives and present the information to them in the way they can best absorb it.

However, the decisive factor is the intention. Whenever your own interests do not fully coincide with those of your counterpart, persuasion can turn into manipulation. However, people usually smell manipulation attempts "three miles upwind".

If we manage to free ourselves from the need to convince, if we allow our counterpart to form their own opinion, we unconsciously send a strong message.

This message is reinforced if you set a good example yourself, if you have the opportunity to pilot the proposal on a small scale and take risks yourself.

Actions are more powerful than words.

If you want to inspire rather than persuade, you can be sure that you will achieve more. By setting a good example, you make your attitude visible.

Chapter 6

THE "SO WHAT"

Why, how and when to start

As a research assistant at the University of Hanover, I have read and evaluated countless diploma, master's and bachelor's theses. I always read the last chapter first. That's why I'm summarizing the most important findings here first.

The most important lessons learned can be summarized as follows:

Marketing expertise is the decisive design element of data analysis for marketing. The equation of correlation and causality is the cardinal error that still unites management and data science today. The dominant hypothesis-driven approach to data analysis has its limits. At best, it produces racing cars that are designed to drive over open, hilly terrain and too often fail.

What is AI? Statistical modeling finds the parameters of a fixed, predetermined formula. Artificial intelligence finds a new, optimized formula, not just its parameters. However, AI suffers from model drift, discrimination and the risk of performing poorly in live operation. Explainable AI does not solve the problem and offers a dangerous false transparency. The solution is called Causal AI. This is for AI like the filter system of a distillery. Ultimately, it is an absolute must.

And this is how you proceed with Causal AI: Start with a "blank sheet of paper" and write down what could influence your target variables. Then obtain the data for this. In addition to internal and external data sources, also consider market research. It offers unique opportunities to understand the inner life of customers.

Model the data with an AI algorithm that ensures in the learning process that predictions are only based on causal causes. Model a causal network, not a pure input-output relationship. Open the AI black box with suitable simulation algorithms. Algorithmically check the causal directions and search for confounders. Optimize your model and recalculate until it is meaningful and useful enough. Finally, standardize everything in one process - from the data, the preparation, the method to the preparation of the results.

Why Causal AI?

AI is present in all marketing processes, be it in insights discovery, operational and strategic decision-making or the generation of marketing content. All of these algorithms suffer from model drift, discrimination and limited reliability of predictions. The risk varies depending on the use case and context. In most cases, Causal AI is a step forward compared to the status without AI. It opens up a new level of development for more performance and less risk.

How to get started?

Find internal allies who are early adopters. They also think about where there is a real problem in the company that Causal AI can solve. Too often we tend to walk around with a belly laugh. "Causal AI can do everything." That confuses and confused people don't make decisions.

A pilot project often makes sense because it carries a limited risk. However, in order to exploit the upside potential, the pilot should be set up in such a way that it serves as a real test case for the rollout and provides clear evidence. If necessary, set a good example and show how you think others should act. Be a role model.

But would you rather wait?

Are you convinced that the cost of the Causal AI Pilot is already less than the benefit? What is the argument for waiting?

Ask yourself how much risk (model drift, discrimination) you can avoid by not waiting. Also ask yourself how big the long-term disadvantage is if you are too late on the learning curve.

If you are an early adopter, these questions are not relevant for you. AI is the value driver of the economy of our time. Causal AI takes AI to new dimensions. The future of AI is "causal".

Causal AI is also and especially an opportunity for marketers not to lose their position in the decision-making process to data science and be unjustly substituted by AI.

Data science needs the expertise of marketers.

Causal AI needs you - as a marketeer and as a human!

ABOUT THE AUTHOR

Dr. Frank Buckler is the founder of Success Drivers, a consultancy for marketing research using Causal AI. He has been researching AI for thirty years, developed the causal AI software NEUSREL as part of his dissertation and later published it in peer-reviewed journals.

Frank Buckler also holds a doctorate in marketing science and spent five years in top management consulting and eight years as head of marketing in a US corporation.

Today he lives with his family in Cologne. You can reach him at Buckler@Success-Drivers.com

Printed in Great Britain
by Amazon